P9-BIE-256

# JACK, YOU'RE FIRED!

The Top 66 Reasons for Firing
Sales Professionals ... And How You
Can Avoid Every Single One Of Them!

## JACK PERRY

McKenna Publishing Group

Jack, You're Fired!


Copyright © 2005 by Jack Perry

All rights reserved. No part of this book may be used or reproduced in any manner
without written permission of McKenna Publishing Group, except in the case of
brief quotations employed in reviews and similar works.

ISBN: 1-932172-18-1
LCCN: 2004106855


Senior editor Diane Armitage
Cover photo by Marc Glassman
Design by Patti Knoles

The Respect Factor is a trademark of Jack Perry.

First Edition
10 9 8 7 6 5 4 3 2 1

Printed in the United States of America

"Jack Perry has determined how to make the first and best sale – to yourself. You'll be a better professional as a result. *Jack, Your Fired!* helps people succeed not fail, collaborate not connive, and see their career as a noble calling, not a game."

Alan Weiss, PhD
Author, *Million Dollar Consulting*
President, Summit Consulting Group, Inc.

"*Jack, You're Fired!* should be required reading for everyone who would like to improve their sales skills and communication skills. Perry focuses on all the important points so necessary to a salesperson's success."

H. Douglas Wood
Chairman, Manulife Wood Logan

"Jack Perry has indeed hit the nail on the head for any sales professional serious about sales success. *Jack, You're Fired!* is truly state-of-the-art and top drawer!"

William T. Brooks
Author, *The New Science of Selling and Persuasion*

"Jack's new book, *Jack, You're Fired!* is a very inspiring, uplifting, easy-to-read manual on how to win in the profession of selling, and how to succeed in the art of life.

Gerhard Gschwandtner
Founder and Publisher *Selling Power*

"There are strategic patterns that allow someone to perform at the highest level, and in this exceptional guide you can learn them from a master. You don't need to be in sales to benefit from Jack Perry's knowledge – the concepts in this book apply to anyone who demands more from themselves and their career."

Anthony Robbins
Author, *Awaken the Giant Within* and *Unlimited Power*
Founder, Robbins Research International

"Every sales professional, sales manager and CEO in the world who chooses to be better organized, have a better life and get improved results should own and use *Jack, You're Fired!*"

Michael Fusco,
Managing Director Private Banking and Investments, Merrill Lynch

"By page two I knew *Jack, You're Fired!* would be a great resource. The secret ... "Successful sales professionals must have the mind set of an owner." What follows is a very practical, easy to read guide that is invaluable to every ambitious sales person. As Jack writes, "Successful sales skills are learned," Why wait? Start reading."

Patricia Fripp
Author of *Get What You Want*
Past President, National Speakers Association

"This is really the ultimate sales workbook ... yet, equally applicable from CEOs to bartenders. We are all sales people, and we all can garner lessons to be learned from Jack's well thought out recommendations. Having worked with many great sales people, including Jack Perry, I can say I do not know anyone who walks their talk more than he does."

Jack Linkletter
Former International President of Young Presidents' Organization

"This book is an amazing guide which must not be missed by sales professionals and CEOs. Jack Perry challenges you with each succinct chapter and then you are shown the paths to improvement and growth...not a cozy and comfortable read...but clearly constructive and full of promise."

Scott Logan
Admiral United States Navy, retired.

"This is a masterful book by an extraordinary executive and professional. It is loaded with substance that can enhance your career and improve your life."

Nido R. Qubein
Chairman, Great Harvest Bread Company
Founder, National Speakers Association Foundation

# TABLE OF CONTENTS

# FOREWORD

"ONCE every couple of years, a book comes along which startles you with its brilliance, elegance and simplicity. Jack Perry's new book is one of those volumes. While it is primarily addressed to the 19 million people who have professional careers in sales or marketing, there is much wisdom in this slim volume from which we can all benefit. Jack Perry has helped the companies for which he has worked (IBM, ManuLife and others) enjoy multi-million dollar increases in sales.

To achieve increases in sales and profits of this magnitude takes more than outstanding products, first rate service and great prices. It takes a team of intelligent, highly trained, energetic and motivated professionals. If you want to be one of the top professionals in your field and operate at peak performance, you will find much value in this remarkable book.

This is a very personal and often entertaining book on developing the personal skills, discipline, attitudes and vision needed to reach the highest levels of success in business and in life. Full of fascinating stories, case studies and insights, this is a book you will want to read several times."

**Donald Moine, Ph.D.**
Business Psychologist
Co-author, *Ultimate Selling Power*

# PREFACE

**NOW,** for the first time ever, through the 66 short "lessons" in this book you have the ability to absolutely BOOM your sales growth in days and weeks ... not years.

In this unique, no-limit profession, the sales professional is the only one-person selection committee when it comes to setting business and personal goals. Congratulations, then, are in order as you've now taken the responsibility to look at your selling skills and take necessary actions to propel your career to the top!

**Permanently brand your mind
with the power of *Jack, You're Fired!***

*Jack, You're Fired!* isn't designed to be read quickly and relegated to a dusty shelf. This unique collection of the top 66 reasons for firing sales professionals is not the Entertainment Hour. *Jack, You're Fired!* is your personal resource, a manual on the truths about the sales profession based on 40-plus years of hard knocks, expensive mistakes, demanding mentors and seized opportunities.

**Let's get started:**
- Truth: It's a myth that sales superstars are born with their skills.
- Truth: Successful sales skills are learned.
- Truth: Successful sales careers are earned.
- Truth: Companies, their sales managers and CEOs endure the expense of far too many failed sales careers.
- Truth: The opportunity for a successful career as a sales professional is available to anyone who chooses to make and keep the commitment.

**How is *Jack, You're Fired!* organized?**
This book is all about Content Power. It is direct and specific. No long stories, boring charts or filler pages. Remember, the

Gettysburg Address had only 10 sentences, comprised of 272 words: brief and to the point, but never forgotten.

You can immediately turn to any topic of personal challenge and, in two or three brief pages, determine if you do, indeed, exhibit characteristics of this problem. You then are given specific solutions that you can begin using today and in the future.

There are 66 chapters, each only a few pages in length. Chapter structure includes:

**Topic**
**Quotation**
**Premise**
**Symptoms of Impending Disaster**
**Relevant story**
**Solutions**
**Results after action is taken**
**P.S. – Points of Wisdom**

## Who Should Read This Book

Who should grab this power tool and put it to profitable use in their life?

- Sales professionals (aka sales consultants)
  - All industries;
  - All experience levels, from the seasoned veteran to the rookie.
- Sales coaches (aka sales managers) who choose to:
  - Increase their team sales;
  - Increase their team members' individual sales;
  - Help their team members achieve greater personal success.
- Sales team support members (aka partners) who choose to:
  - Improve their selling skills;
  - Help their sales team partners increase sales;
  - Increase company sales and profits.
- CEOs (aka leaders) who seek:
  - Increased sales of their company's products and/or services;
  - Greater productivity from their sales team;

- Increased company profits.
· Anyone who chooses to advance his or her proposals
  and ideas.

### Here's How To Make This Book Work For You

Take just **5 simple steps** to improve your sales performance immediately and enjoy your day-to-day opportunities in this no-limit profession.

### 1. Personal Sales Skill Audit

Turn to the back of *Jack, You're Fired!* and complete your Personal Sales Skill Audit. This Audit involves 66 questions representing the 66 chapters in this book. Your candid answers will help you immediately focus your energies on necessary areas of improvement.

### 2. Begin

This unique sales tool does not have a traditional beginning and ending. You have the option of starting with Chapter One or you may turn directly to the chapters that more specifically address your issues and needs.

Like it or not, every sales professional, regardless of success and experience, will find at least one self-descriptive trait in these pages – and probably more! Fortunately, you will also find step-by-step support and action opportunities to eliminate certain behaviors, attitudes, dated misconceptions and time-consuming dodges that build giant barriers against reaching one's sales goals.

### 3. Study

Thoroughly study each chapter in *Jack, You're Fired!* and incorporate the rules outlined there into your daily sales behavior. Be vigilant.

### 4. Action Plan

After studying each chapter, decide on any specific action plan you choose to take for focused self-improvement. Go to the end of *Jack, You're Fired!* and review **My Sales Act Report**. This free sales tool is available at http://www.respectfactor.com.

The **Sales Act Report** keeps you on target and serious about taking the necessary action and obtaining improved results.

### Accountability

You have the opportunity to invite someone to hold you personally accountable for your individually chosen plans of action, the changes you choose to make. Ask your sales coach, a friend or mentor to help you. Give them a copy of your completed Sales Act Report, and periodically review this working paper with your partner.

### Revisit

As needed, revisit the content-rich *Jack, You're Fired!* and give yourself a tune-up.

### Share

Share your expertise with your team members. When you teach, you reinforce your own knowledge. This is a proven fact.

## 5. Stay on Course for Exponential Success

Go to the internet and bookmark www.respectfactor.com for quick access to new, actionable ideas.

### Stay Focused

Go to www.respectfactor.com and sign up for the free Respect Factor quote of the week; this is specifically chosen by Jack Perry with a compatible action step.

### Rely On Expertise

Go to www.respectfactor.com to subscribe to the **free Respect Factor e-zine**, written by Jack Perry.

### Increase Knowledge

Increase your professional knowledge by learning from the value-added articles available at www.respectfactor.com.

*"Everyone everyday is selling: an idea, a concept, an agreement, a service, a product and most importantly yourself."*
*— Jack Perry*

With **Jack, You're Fired!** you'll become consciously aware of the key issues that bring many sales professionals crashing down, and how you can successfully counteract those career killers for a long-term career of rocketing, exponential success!

Thanks for your trust and confidence.
**Jack Perry**

P.S. I will see you in the Winners' Circle.

# MIND-SET

# OWNERSHIP

## The Power of Thinking Like an Owner, Not an Employee

*"When it comes to betting on yourself, you're a
chicken-livered coward if you hesitate."* — B.C. Forbes

### Premise:

Successful sales professionals must have a mind-set of an owner. How would your daily routine change if you saw your name on the door, – Jack Perry, Inc. – and if your name were on the company checks? How would you act if you were the president or sales manager? Well, you can have it that way if you think that way. Consider asking yourself each morning, "What does it take to earn and get the business that's in the best interest of the client and the prospect?" As an owner, there are no Start and Stop times in your day and week. There are no more "have-tos," and the word "work" has been eliminated from your vocabulary and replaced with "opportunity" and "ownership."

Owners get paid for solutions. Hourly workers get a coffee break.

### Symptoms of Impending Disaster:

- You watch the clock for time to take coffee and lunches.
- You rarely stay late or work on weekends.
- You manifest an Us (sales team) vs. Them (sales management) attitude.
- You don't really take ownership of ideas and suggestions.
- You often grumble behind the management's back about implementation of the company decisions.
- Invariably, you are asking the question, "What's in it for me?"
- In your mind, the phrase "long-term" is the next payday.

### Story:

At ManuLife Wood Logan, our Santa Barbara office manager was a young man with great potential by the name of Jeff Olsen. Jeff talked about being an entrepreneur but, up to this point, had not had an experience as such. I told Jeff to take the following action:

"Some day, when everyone has left the office, take a big piece of paper and print in big, bold print, the following: Jeff Olsen, Inc.

"Take it out to the front door, and tape it there. Stand back and stare at it. Let that picture burn into your mind: the imprint of your own company. This is Jeff's firm. Now, how would you run it differently once inside those doors?"

Jeff bought the idea and is now managing a very successful sales territory that, in his mind, is his own company.

## Solutions:

1. Your owner's mind-set will see you making different decisions and working with a new kind of enthusiasm, a new perspective.
2. Put up a sign at your home office that says, "Jack Perry, Inc." or, if you're married, get your spouse involved with a buy-in: "Judy and Jack Perry, Inc." This will keep your mind-set focused on thinking and acting like an owner.
3. In self-talk, refer to yourself as the president, the vice president, or the sales manager.
4. Think and act bottom-line profit.
5. Share your owner mind-set with your clients and prospects.
6. If a problem develops, ask yourself: How would the owner solve this?

## Results:

1. There are no more "have-to's" in your sales career.
2. Your selling opportunity will no longer just be a job.
3. You will visualize your opportunities in sales from quite a different viewpoint.
4. You will never question the time, energy and resources you invest in your business.
5. Your activity and sales numbers will increase because you're investing more of yourself in YOUR business.
6. You will feel and experience greater control.
7. You will have a focused purpose: building your business.

**P.S.** Ownership rewards you with dividends.

# COMMITMENT

## The Power of Making a Commitment

*"The quality of a person's life is in direct proportion to their commitment, regardless of their chosen field of endeavor." — Vincent T. Lombardi*
*The legendary former coach of the Superbowl champions, the Green Bay Packers*

**Premise:**

Commitment brings out the best in you because it forces you to focus on your personal agreements with yourself. A commitment is a pledge or a promise; it's keeping your word and walking your talk. Commitment is doing what you said you would do. Having grown up in a small agricultural town in Southern California on the Mexican border where my Dad was a ranch foreman, I quickly learned that your word was your bond. When you shook hands, it was a commitment. You didn't need a signed contract.

**Symptoms of Impending Disaster:**

- You squirm when being asked to make a commitment.
- Breaking appointments comes too easily to you.
- Your consistency in breaking commitments is resulting in clients, prospects and peers not being able to rely on you.
- You have a long trail of projects that you have discarded long before completion because you didn't make the full commitment.
- You find that when the going gets tough, you allow yourself to give your second-best effort and don't stretch to do your best.
- When your sales management team needs a commitment for a special project, it looks elsewhere.
- You commit to making more sales calls but frequently choose to quit before you meet your target.
- It doesn't bother your conscience when you break a commitment.
- You frequently break commitments to your clients and prospects. Service requests are late, answers to questions are not timely, and missed appointments occur too often.

- You don't keep your commitment to timely communication with your sales management and sales support team.

## Story:

In 1997, in Sun Valley, Idaho, a neighbor of mine wanted to sell his home and move back to his ranch. Sun Valley was getting too big for him – granted, a population of only 1,200 – but it was just too big for him. My neighbor asked that I help him in the listing process, and I agreed. We established a relationship with a broker in town and listed Charlie's fine home. I knew it would sell; it was a beautiful place right on the river.

Late one afternoon, I got the call to bring Charlie into the office because they had a buyer for his home. After listening to the presentation late that afternoon, Charlie agreed to the terms and shook hands with the real estate broker. The broker looked at her watch and said, "It's late in the day. Can we sign the papers tomorrow?" "Sure, no problem," was Charlie's reply.

Well, news travels fast in a small town. That night, Charlie received a call from another broker who offered him $55,000 more with an immediate cash sale. What do you think Charlie said? "No thanks. Being raised on a farm, we all lived by our word. I made a commitment; I gave my word. The original offer is a done deal."

## Solutions:

1. Get real. Understand what commitment means.
2. When asked for a commitment, wake up to the fact that you're being asked to make a decision and follow through with action. Pause for a moment and ask yourself, "Is this a commitment I'm willing to make?" then move forward with a "Yes" or a "No."
3. Go to a true friend as well as a trusted business associate and ask both for the truth on your commitment scorecard.
4. Put commitment into play in your everyday life, starting with

the person who you should make the greatest commitment to: yourself.

5.  Start with personal life values and commitments that include:
    a.  Your health: exercise and food consumption
    b.  Your mind: positive thinking
    c.  Your family: relationship building
    d.  Your community: volunteerism/service
    e.  Your charities
6.  Now, move on to bigger sales success commitments: i.e. sales activity and sales numbers.
7.  Make your sales and prospecting target numbers public and, therefore, maintain your accountability.
8.  Each time you break a commitment, examine why this occurred and how you will avoid repeating it in the future.
9.  Steer clear of people who are chronic commitment breakers. They are not accountable.
10. Take pride in being a commitment master.

**Results:**
1.  When asked for a commitment and you consider it and make it, you will now keep it.
2.  Clients and prospects will know they can count on you.
3.  When a client or prospect is stuck and needs quick assistance, he will turn to you.
4.  Increased responsibilities will come your way because of your reputation as a commitment keeper.
5.  You will attract commitment-oriented people to you.
6.  You will receive greater results in every aspect of your life by making the commitments for your body, your mind, your family, your community and your business.
7.  You will feel good about yourself because you are walking your talk.

**P.S.** Without a commitment, you're destined to settle for mediocrity – a safe and bland middle ground. No thanks! Go for the gold with commitments.

# ATTITUDE

## Your Attitude Needs More Altitude

*"The greatest discovery of my generation is that a human being can alter his life by altering his attitude."* — William James

**Premise:**

Attitude is the dominant controlling factor to all happiness and success. The good news: It's 100% your choice. It's as simple as deciding that you "can do" rather than "can not." Your positive mind-set will influence every aspect of your life. You will move toward that which you dwell upon. People love degrees and the most important degree is a PMA (Positive Mental Attitude). Your attitude is actually more important than your aptitude.

**Symptoms of Impending Disaster:**

- You find yourself frequently giving negative responses in your conversations.
- Your glass is always half empty in terms of how you see situations in life.
- Someone or some situation always seems to be raining on your parade.
- You can't find it in yourself to enjoy other people's success.
- You find yourself hanging around with negative people because it's easier to swap stories with losers and receive their negative support.
- You make fun of people who are always positive and look to the bright side of life.

**Story:**

When Judy and I lived in Sun Valley, Idaho, I would occasionally take a ten-minute walk along Trail Creek into town for an early breakfast with the locals – they were a colorful and fun bunch. The favorite hangout, The Kneadery, had tasty food, giant portions, real people, a pioneer-town atmosphere, and tender loving care from the wait staff. The waitresses made it all happen. They would greet you with a cheerful, "Good morning, Jack, what's happening? What can I do for you?"

From there, they'd remember key details of your life, i.e. "How is Judy? I bet her garden is in full bloom. Have you hiked to Pioneer Cabin this season?" You didn't have a chance for a sour attitude.

It was a very simple formula and it worked. All of us literally threw handfuls of money and compliments at these wonderful mavens of attitude.

**Solutions:**
1. Every day, look for the good in daily events.
2. As Zig Ziglar says, "You must get rid of that stinking thinking."
3. Every time you catch yourself saying something negative or interpreting something negative, be proactive, turn it around and respond in a positive manner.
4. Always look for the big plus in people.
5. Seek out people who have positive attitudes, simply because they're happier.
6. As you greet people, give them your big, warm smile.

**Results:**
1. As your attitude turns positive, people will begin to respond more favorably to you.
2. With a positive attitude, you will see more possibilities in every aspect of your life.
3. You will be happier and feel much better about yourself as an individual and, in turn, will positively impact everyone in your world.
4. Positive people attract positive people. This is one case where opposites don't attract.
5. You will immediately respond to any potentially negative sales issue with a solution to turn it into a positive.
6. Your clients and prospects will see more possible uses of your products and services.

7. You are like a bee pollinating the flowers, with your PMA. You will also make your clients' and prospects' day.
8. You will help your clients and prospects be more positive in their lives.

**P.S.** Build your long-term sales success on a rock-solid foundation of positive attitude.

# INTEGRITY

## Your Honor Code Will Put You on the High Road

*"I would prefer to fail with honor than win by cheating."*
— Sophocles

**Premise:**

Always take the high road. Honesty and commitment are the moral codes of living. It is a choice that we all can make. At some point in our lives, certain mentors, parents, and business associates influence our respective choices regarding our integrity code. The key becomes adherence to your chosen code of living. Your friends, clients and prospects don't expect perfection, but they do expect timely, candid and honest communications. In the book, *The Millionaire Mind*, author Thomas J. Stanley lists integrity as the number one reason for millionaires' economic success. When you practice integrity in your business and personal life, you will experience greater personal and business satisfaction and results.

**Symptoms of Impending Disaster:**

- Occasionally, you add a few extra miles on your expense form knowing you work for a big company and they won't miss it.
- You think it's OK that members of your political party stretch the truth in pursuit of an election.
- You choose not to tell all the downsides of your respective product or service as it relates to the successful use by your clients and prospects.
- You mislead your clients and prospects regarding service expectation.
- You blame your sales support staff for your errors.
- You cheat on your income tax.
- You don't tell your sales manager when you make a mistake.
- You occasionally tell a white lie to get out of a personal commitment.
- You don't feel guilty regarding your occasional dishonesty.

- You talk behind your manager's back.
- You think you're above the law.

**Story:**

Sadly, two of America's former presidents each made a serious mistake and then compounded it by lying about it; they didn't come clean fast enough for the American people. In the real world – especially in America – people are very forgiving with timely, candid and honest people. Perhaps if President Richard Nixon and President Bill Clinton had each immediately acknowledged the problem, admitted their error and asked for forgiveness, they would not have suffered permanent and humiliating embarrassment – Nixon was asked to resign, Clinton was impeached by the House and acquitted by the Senate, yet they are still branded, their record and legacy tarnished forever.

Doug Wood, a founder of ManuLife Wood Logan, put it this way: "If there is any doubt, there is no doubt."

**Solutions:**

1. Never blame others for your errors.
2. Come fast with bad news.
3. Keep clients and prospects informed regarding any challenges.
4. Accept the fact that you will make mistakes. Don't try to cover them up.
5. If facts change, tell all the people who will be impacted immediately.
6. Give your clients and prospects the best advice, even if it means saying that the competitor's product has superior benefits.
7. Live your life with an unchanging moral code.

**Results:**

1. You'll like yourself better.
2. You will experience less time and energy wasted through fabricating stories.
3. Clients and prospects will respect your commitment to being timely, candid and honest.

4. Your trust will grow in the eyes of the clients and prospects.
5. You will attract friends who are similar in moral code and integrity.
6. People will share their confidences with you knowing you won't misuse the information.
7. You will develop a reputation as a professional with integrity.

**P.S.** Remember, it is the person in the mirror who counts. Aristotle said, "Integrity is everything."

# LOYALTY

## Has Your Loyalty Sunken Like a Lead Balloon?

*"A man who will steal for me will steal from me."*
*— Teddy Roosevelt*

**Premise:**

We certainly want our friends, family and fellow team members to be loyal to us. Without being loyal yourself, how can you expect consistent loyalty from your sales manager, fellow sales team members, clients, prospects and friends? Perhaps loyalty is like a pregnancy: You cannot be a little pregnant, and you cannot be a little loyal. It's all or nothing. Use loyalty as the cornerstone for your trust foundation with your clients, prospects and friends. When you are part of a sales team and enjoy the associated benefits, always support it, or move on and let another loyal individual wear that coveted jersey.

**Symptoms of Impending Disaster:**

- You're only loyal when it is to your advantage.
- You become indignant when clients and prospects aren't loyal to you, but you don't question yourself when your loyalty does flip-flops.
- When someone speaks poorly of your friends, you just nod your head, don't respond and don't defend your friend. We call that two-faced.
- You frequently catch yourself talking out of both sides of your mouth. Such behavior makes for a big mouth.
- You smile and compliment your sales manager in personal conversations and then join in knocking him or her when you're with other sales team members.
- You knock the company you are with, even though they gave you a start when you couldn't even spell "sales."
- You invest more time and research in new prospects and neglect your loyal and good customers.

**Story:**

In 1960, I joined the IBM sales team in Los Angeles, and was introduced to their strict, professional business dress code. In need of a quick fix, I acted on a tip from my friend, Ross, and took a trip to see Guy Livingston, the owner of a prominent local men's clothing store. Guy's advice was timely and candid. When I walked into the office the following week in my new blue suit, I felt as if I were 10 feet tall.

Over the years, Guy provided excellent service – sending clothes to me overnight, doing last-minute alterations, and more. As a result, for more than 40 years, I purchased virtually 100% of my wardrobe from the same store without shopping the competitors.

**Solutions:**

1. Honor loyalty as a fundamental trait and take pride in it.
2. Speak up when loyalty is an issue.
3. Don't remain silent and allow someone to speak poorly regarding a friend.
4. Distance yourself from disloyal people.
5. Compliment your friends and associates who publicly demonstrate their loyalty to products, service, and friends.
6. Always maintain allegiance to your firm.
7. Take care of your loyal customers first.

**Results:**

1. You will find yourself around like-minded people who value loyalty.
2. Your sales managers will give you the benefit of the doubt if there is ever an issue.
3. You will like yourself better.
4. You will get extra opportunities because of your loyalty.
5. Your clients and prospects will respect and reward your loyalty.

**P.S.** Bob Cassato, president of Manulife Wood Logan, has a favorite saying when it comes to loyalty: "Short resume, long net worth – long resume, short net worth."

# TRUST

## How to Build Trust to Create Clients for Life

*"To make a buying decision, the customer has to make a leap of faith. Successful sales people create a safety net called 'trust.' Trust helps your customers take that leap with confidence."* — Gerhard Gschwandtner

### Premise:

People buy from people. Certainly there are occasions when someone walks in the door and gives you the order because you were in the right place at the right time. For long-term professional sales success, however, you must build foundations of trust with your clients and prospects based on your actions. Trust is the bulwark of lasting relationships. In essence, trust is founded on events happening between people.

### Symptoms of Impending Disaster:

- You don't trust your sales manager and company.
- You notice that your clients and prospects are not volunteering helpful information.
- When you have a misunderstanding with clients or prospects, they never seem to give you the benefit of the doubt.
- Upon reflection, you notice that you have few, if any, truly close personal friends.
- Your sales manager doesn't review critical ideas with you for your input prior to telling your teammates.
- You continually say, "Trust me," in your conversations – a bad sign.
- You basically do not trust other people.
- You frequently break your word.
- Your follow-up is lousy.
- You think it's only the promise that counts and not the delivery.
- Clients and prospects cannot trust your answers.
- You cannot keep confidential matters confidential.

### Story:

On the weekends and in the summer, I always enjoyed going

with my Dad to the farm supply center. When Dad, who was the ranch manager, ordered fertilizer, seed and equipment, there was never a signature, a contract or a traditional agreement signed. Dad and the supply center manager merely shook hands, looked each other in the eye and said, "It's a deal." It simply was the way business was done in small agricultural communities when you had to rely on each other for your success and your future. Dad said, "Your word is your bond."

**Solutions:**
1. Take a trust audit.
   a. List the people who trust you and why they trust you.
   b. List those people you trust and why.
2. List the keys to building trust from your viewpoint: keeping your word, no gossip, delivering your promises.
3. Always make good on any errors.
4. If you make a mistake, immediately go public and tell people.
5. Be aware of trust-destroying or trust-building during your day-to-day communications.
6. Review your promises.
7. Tell the entire story regarding your products and services – the pluses and minuses.

**Results:**
1. More people will turn to you for advice.
2. Your management team will share sensitive information with you, looking for your input.
3. You will start to trust other people.
4. You will receive increased loyalty from your clients and prospects.
5. Your client and prospect relationships will go to the next level almost of their own accord.
6. Sales professionals who are viewed by clients and prospects as trustworthy will receive favorable attention.

**P.S.** Thanks for your trust and confidence!

# DIRECTION

# MISSION STATEMENT

### Your Mission is Missing:  Here is How to Find It

*"If our ladder is not leaning against the right wall, every step we take, no matter how many hours we prepared for it, gets us to the wrong place."*
*— Stephen Covey*

**Premise:**

Given a chance, serious sales professionals choose direction and focus. Without a mission statement, you are a ship without a rudder. Your mission must be clearly written down and posted for all to see. If it isn't written down, you did not think it out, nor will you be able to remain on target. A mission statement imprints itself on your brain and helps reduce all the distracting noise around you.

**Symptoms of Impending Disaster:**
- Your mission statement isn't written.
- When pressed for an answer, you choose to verbalize your mission statement.
- You seem to change your mission statement the same way you change your socks – daily.
- Your clients and prospects don't have a clue as to what your mission statement is about.
- You are not fired up over your mission statement.
- You believe that mission statements are for the boss, MBAs, and giant corporations and that sales professionals don't need them.

**Story:**

In my opinion, the phenomenal success of Starbucks is no accident. One thing that has clearly helped their success is their carefully-crafted mission statement.

The Starbucks' mission statement puts people first and profits in last place. After preparing their mission statement, Starbucks took the extra step to ensure that the company walked its talk. They established a "Mission Review Team" to monitor their real practices against their mission statement. Pocket-sized comment cards are available to every employee to report to the team if he or she is aware of a decision or behavior that doesn't support the mission statement. As a result, employees are involved in actually living the mission statement and possess a greater sense of being part of the team.

Now, let's have a cup of coffee and talk about your mission statement.

## Solutions:

1. Accept the fact that a mission statement can give your career specific purpose and direction.
2. Ask other successful professionals to share their mission statements with you.
3. Obtain the mission statements from successful companies. Check out Southwest Airlines' mission statement, noticing that it reflects their position in the marketplace and their success. Is it just a coincidence that their stock has been one of the most successful stocks on the New York Stock Exchange in the past several years?
4. Read Stephen Covey's guidelines on establishing a mission statement. You'll find it in his book, *7 Habits of Highly Successful People*. Covey's personal mission statement is less than ten words.
5. Be specific in your mission statement.
6. Review it; get input. Test it out on friends and clients.
7. Publish it for all to see.
8. Now, go out and live by it.

## Results:

1. There will be no question about your career direction and purpose.
2. Clients and prospects will be able to recite your mission statement back to you and to your friends and your prospects.
3. You'll have improved focus on your energy and resources.
4. You will attract clients that relate to your mission statement, and

avoid those that don't. This will help you achieve your mission.

5.   You will be in control of your career.

**P.S.** Ensure your success with a well-defined road map – your personal mission statement. Sarah Victory, the author of *How to Double Your Business In One Year Or Less,* put it on the line when she said, "How would I change the world if I were the ruler or emporer for the day?" Now go out and make your own world.

# GOALS

## How to Not Just Set, but Also ACHIEVE Major Goals

*"This one step — choosing a goal and staying to it —*
*changes everything." — Scott Reed*

**Premise:**

You will move toward what you dwell upon: in essence, your goals. We all have goals: to earn a place on an athletic team, achieve specific grades in school, be selected for a job promotion, get into great physical condition, win a sales contest or exceed our sales activity targets. The key to accomplishing goals is the discipline to take control of the goal-setting and implementing processes to make them work for you. With established goals and action plans, you have direction in your life. Your goals are your dreams with action steps and time deadlines.

**Symptoms of Impending Disaster:**

- You love to talk about your dreams over and over again.
- You poke fun at those people who set their goals and never achieve them, even though they do seem to experience success along the way.
- Your sales manager has asked you to set higher income goals but you dance around the issue and choose not to do so.
- You're afraid to set big goals because of fear of failure.
- You have a very hazy focus on your objectives.

**Story:**

In 1970, Hiram W. Smith, one of the founders of the Franklin Covey organization, accepted the challenge of turning around a Boy Scout Explorer troop floundering due to bad attitudes and no direction. He began by challenging them to set a goal. He said, "I'm going to Hawaii next summer with my wife. If you would like to raise the money through various fund-raising projects you, too, can join us. The first step in the process is to memorize a poem by Ella

Wheeler Wilcox."

The short poem goes as follows:

*"Will"*

*There is no chance ... no destiny ... no fate that can circumvent or hinder or control the firm resolve of a determined soul.*

Each Wednesday at the troop meeting, each member of the troop was asked to stand and recite the poem.

Fast forward to the end of the year, when they had raised more than enough money to pay for their trip to Hawaii. As they boarded the airplane for Hawaii, each Boy Scout stood in front of the flight attendant and repeated the poem. It's very simple: Nothing can stop the determined soul.

**Solutions:**

1. List your goals by category: family, business, personal health, community, financial, and spiritual.
2. Write them out.
3. Establish a time period (short, medium and long-term) for each of the above goals.
4. Categorize your goals in sequence (high to low) in order of their importance to you.
5. Prepare written affirmations regarding the goals that you choose to work on at this time.
6. In quick review, the rules for creating an affirmation consists of the following:
   a. First person
   b. Present tense
   c. Positive
   d. Something you choose to bring about in your life. Example: "I take great pride in exceeding my sales activity targets each and every week."
7. Recite each affirmation at a minimum of twice each day, with your eyes closed, visualizing every part of that goal.
8. Think big!

**Results:**

1.  You will experience the satisfaction of knowing you've established a direction in life with each of your goals.
2.  You will experience less wasted energy and resources.
3.  You will expand your vision of success.
4.  Your confidence will soar as you accomplish your goals, and set new ones.
5.  You will increase your sales activity, your sales, and your income.
6.  You will feel in control.

**P.S.** When you get in your car in the morning, and don't have a destination in mind, any road will get you where you want to go. Prepare a road map with your goals and live the journey of your dreams.

# PLANNING

## If You are Going in All Directions, You May Soon be Going Out the Door!

*"Good plans shape good decisions. That's why good planning helps to make elusive dreams come true." — Lester Bittle*

**Premise:**

A home is generally considered the major asset for most Americans. When you build a house, you plan the concept, and then draw the plans. Then you finalize the plans. And then you implement the plans – it's a logical sequence. Remember, your sales career provides the resources for that house, as well as your lifestyle and your retirement. Don't you think a comprehensive plan to implement your sales career success would further ensure that very success? You bet! Without a plan, don't plan on having success.

**Symptoms of Impending Disaster:**
- You take your sales manager's requests very lightly when he asks for your business plan.
- Your plan is really just a copy of last year's business plan with a few cosmetic updates.
- You rarely refer back to your business plan.
- During the weeks and months of the year, your plan lives permanently in a file drawer, collecting dust.
- Your plan is too complicated to be used effectively and monitored frequently.
- You spend more time planning your vacations than you do planning your sales career.
- Your goal achievement is sporadic at best.
- You're running your business by default.

**Story:**

During the late 1980s in Laguna Beach, California, we were faced with a financial disaster in our schools. A group of concerned parents met in our home and formed a non-profit foundation for the benefit of the local schools. One afternoon, my wife, Judy, recommended the name, "SchoolPower," which we adopted and then went after the local community to gift money back into the school system as an investment in our children.

We mapped out the city geographically and assigned a specific number of residences to each of our team captains to call. As to the businesses, we looked for centers of influence, and assigned team captains to call and ask for help. It was an immediate success, raising over $100,000 in our first year. SchoolPower continues to provide significant financial assistance to the public school system there in Laguna Beach – and all because we started with a very specific plan.

## Solutions:
1. Start today planning for tomorrow.
2. Ask others if they will allow you to review their plans.
3. Write your plan down, look at it and do it.
4. Have a one-year and a three-year plan.
5. Get resource material from the library, the Internet, and the bookstore that will help you in the creation of your plan.
6. Begin with the end in mind as discussed in Stephen Covey's bestseller *7 Habits of Highly Effective People.*
7. Check back on a periodic basis for focus and course correction.

## Results:
1. You will experience less anxiety because you now have a direction.
2. You will experience better utilization of your time, energy and resources.
3. You can say "no" to potential opportunities if they do not fit into your plan.
4. You will have more time for your truly important items.
5. You will be in control of your destiny.

6.  You will spend time and resources with the correct clients and prospects.

**P.S.** "If you don't know where you're going, you'll end up someplace else." – Yogi Berra

# IN PERSON

# APPEARANCE

## Your Image Needs More Power and Prestige

*"Dress to win." — Jack Perry*

**Premise:**

People buy from people and, in the process, they deal with opinions, bias and experience. The total you is the package — not just your product knowledge, degrees and communication skills. Remember the old adage: You never get a second chance for a first impression. You might also say that you get to make a first impression only once. Show your clients and prospects that you pay very close attention to your personal appearance, details, and your client relationships.

**Symptoms of Impending Disaster:**

- Each morning when you go into your closet, you put on the first thing that comes into view.
- Your hair needs to be cut.
- Those pants were obviously made too small, because they're a little tight around the waist.
- Your suit looks as if you slept in it on the train.
- Your shoes could belong to a commando in a recent Marine invasion.
- Your neckties are from your Dad's generation.
- The spots on your necktie resemble those of a Dalmatian dog.
- When traveling on an airplane, you think you're invisible and, therefore, wear clothes that look as if they came from a thrift shop.
- You are never pointed to as an example of a well-dressed professional.
- When you put on your clothes and look in the mirror, there's little reason why people would look at you and say, "Wow! Now, there's a professional!"

**Story:**

When I joined IBM in 1960, my wardrobe was half college days and, since I grew up on a ranch, half farm boy. Yes, I did have a suit and "a" means singular. I quickly got the message and also got the treatment. Early every morning, before the business day began, I met with my training coordinator, Ann Ratichek, who was responsible for reviewing and critiquing my professional dress. She had the power to fire me and I knew it.

While she put fear in my heart, she also helped me steer successfully through the appearance requirements at IBM. In those days, "Big Blue's" uniform of the day was a dark suit, white shirt and shined shoes. To this day, I pay very careful attention to my wardrobe and all aspects of my grooming.

While having a breakfast team meeting one morning with Tom Watson, Jr., he said, "Jack, you don't ever want to do anything with your dress that could cost you a client or prospect."

**Solutions:**
1. Take pride in your personal appearance.
2. Every morning when you get up and stand in front of that mirror, ask the pivotal question: "Would I do business with me?" Be serious. Be honest. Be harsh. If the answer is "no," quickly jump back into bed for the day.
3. Carefully observe the good appearances and the poor appearances in your teammates and competitors.
4. Find good clothing consultants and take their advice.
5. Consider tailor-made clothes. You'll find they feel just like the success you have with a tailor-made presentation.
6. When choosing your wardrobe, commit to quality rather than quantity. It pays.
7. There are books, classes and consultants that will help you quickly and easily improve and change your appearance. No more excuses. Find a reference and start applying it.
8. Every four months review your wardrobe.

9. Have your clothes laid out and ready for action the night before.
10. Commit to investing in your appearance.

**Results:**
1. Because of your professional dress, your clients and prospects will assume that you're a professional in all other matters.
2. When you look in the mirror every morning, you'll truly like what you see and customers and prospects will like what they see.
3. The compliments from your clients, prospects and sales team members will pour in. Your self-esteem takes an uptick.
4. Your clients will choose you to present to their decision-makers.
5. The competition will sit up and take notice.
6. When you enter a room, heads will turn.

**P.S.** Don't challenge the fact that people will judge you by the way you appear in public. Get serious about your appearance.

# LIKEABLE

## People Like People Who Like People:
## The Power of Being Likeable

*"All other things being equal, the more likeable sales professional will win the day." — Jack Perry*

**Premise:**

No. All people in this world are NOT created equal. Yes. The art of being instantly likeable by your customers and prospects can be learned. When you're easily and instantly likeable, you will always have a head start in sales. When the score is close regarding who gets the business, the charisma card has more than just face value. Certainly, some of us have had better mentors than others when it comes to the skills needed to win, and win big, in the sales profession. This shouldn't stop any of us from seeking mentorship in this regard, and climbing the steps to the #1 spot in likeability.

**Symptoms of Impending Disaster:**

- At social gatherings, people you've just met quickly excuse themselves from the conversation.
- When you look in the mirror, you see no smile or spark or evidence of likeability.
- You tell yourself that the facts count, and you don't think it's important that people like you.
- You've never defined what it takes to be a likeable person.
- Upon reflection, you are not sure which of your customers or prospects really like you.
- Your clients and prospects never invite you to their social events.
- You don't have any real friends among your clients or prospects.
- The first impression you give to other people is not good.
- You don't particularly like your customers or prospects; you see them just as a source of income.

**Story:**

In our community, there's certainly more than a single grocery store, but my dear wife, Judy, definitely avoids one of the better stores because one of the checkers is a walking bad attitude. My wife says, "She's just unpleasant to be around. She always complains, never has a good word, and knocks the management team. I'd rather drive two miles further and deal with a smiling, affable checker from Jensen's." In this case, both stores offer a basic commodity, but one wins the business because of the likeability factor. Judy has made a buying decision and will also send her friends to that more likeable store.

**Solutions:**
1. Start by taking a look at your friends and acquaintances and ask yourself why you like them. Then, at the opposite end, when you meet certain people, why does your internal steel curtain go down?
2. Ask your friends and managers whom they consider to be instantly likeable. Watch and learn from them, and ask "Why?"
3. Seek out as friends the people who are universally liked. You'll learn a great deal by being around them.
4. See how many people you can get to smile back at you every day.
5. Set a goal to make one new friend every day.
6. Make it a self-directed game and strategy of getting your toughest prospects to like you.
7. Import likeability traits into your everyday life.
8. Start by liking yourself.
9. Every day, work at the art of making good first impressions. Connect with others.

**Results:**
1. You will get off to a positive start when first meeting clients, prospects and peers.
2. You will win over some tough prospects because they can't say "No" forever – not when they like you.

3. You will make personal friends with some of your clients and prospects.
4. Your support team will give you extra help because you are genuinely liked.
5. You will receive more unsolicited referrals because your customers and prospects truly like you.

**P.S.** Start each morning by looking in the mirror, smiling and saying, "I like me, and so do all my clients and prospects."

# AUTHENTIC

## You Need to Learn the Power of Being Yourself

*"This, above all: To thine own self be true, and it must follow as the night the day, you canst not then be false to any man." — William Shakespeare*

### Premise:

As in art and jewelry, imitations are always less valuable than the original. You and your clients, prospects and friends can quickly see and smell a phony. Clients and prospects want the truth; they are only interested in dealing with real people. Don't pretend to be someone else. Make sure you consistently project the real you, knowing that not everyone will like you. That's OK – enough people will. Don't be afraid to be distinctive, different, and a true individual. Don't forget who you are.

### Symptoms of Impending Disaster:

- You're always taking a survey for the current insight or popular view on sensitive subjects.
- You're afraid to express your true feelings to clients and prospects.
- When asked for a choice, you parrot others and never give your own views.
- You're really not sure who you are.
- You tend to copy everyone else's persona.
- You're not a brand – you're a confused collage of other individuals.
- You hide behind a curtain and don't let people know the real you.
- You are trying to please everyone.

### Story:

Today, Tony Alessandra is recognized as a respected public speaker and a true expert in his field. In his beginning years, when Tony was transitioning from being a college professor to public speaker, he teamed up with Jim Cathcart who was, and is, one of the speaking industry's very best.

As Tony pursued excellence in his career, he engaged Bill Gove, the first president of the National Speaker's Association and a speaking coach. After watching Tony on the platform, Bill told Tony that he was obviously trying to be a duplicate of his friend, Cathcart. Gove told Tony, "You will never make it." He further told Tony to develop the impish Italian street kid that he once was, and be the real thing. Tony took Gove's advice and his speaking career started to soar. Tony was now being Tony, not trying to be Jim Cathcart. Tony is now his own Best Self. Strive for your own Best Self.

## Solutions:

1. Look in the mirror and ask, "Who am I?" Then listen very carefully to your answer.
2. List your values on paper by category in all facets of your life: family, religion, career/work, children and more.
3. When asked a question, think and then always give your answer, not someone else's answer.
4. Open up and let your clients and prospects know and experience the real you.
5. Dump the phony facades.
6. Take pride in being you. You are unique.

## Results:

1. You won't be confused as to who you are.
2. Your clients and prospects will confide in you.
3. You'll like yourself better.
4. You'll have fewer sales opportunities that will be string-alongs, i.e., a lot of conversation and no payday.
5. You will develop lasting personal relationships with your clients and prospects.
6. Being authentic is one of the basic elements of building trust and sales opportunities.
7. You will attract authentic people to you.
8. Now that you are no longer acting like someone else, you will use your energy and resources toward developing the YOU into a unique sales professional.

# ETIQUETTE

## Your Manners are Missing-in-Action

*"Good manners will open doors that the best education cannot."*
*— Charles Thomas*

**Premise:**

Your social graces play an important role in your relationships. Etiquette counts and should be on display for everyone, including your boss, clients and prospects. People everywhere, including your boss and your clients, notice and make judgments regarding your manners and social graces, or lack thereof. People subconsciously grade the conduct of their fellow man. When it comes to manners, you can ace the test and get an "A+" if you choose. Good manners are timeless.

**Symptoms of Impending Disaster:**

- You think social graces are only important to the high society Vanderbilt crowd.
- Sometimes you default to the manners you used in your high school cafeteria days – a real "Animal House."
- You're awkward with introductions; you might not be sure who gets introduced to whom.
- You sit while others stand when a woman enters a room, or is seated at your table.
- At a formal dinner, you look at your utensils as if they were a puzzle. You don't have any idea which eating utensil to use or how to use it.
- You never respond to an invitation. You just arrive.
- You think it takes too much time and energy to send out written thank-you notes.

**Story:**

On Wall Street during an educational seminar, four of us were having breakfast before the day's meetings. A woman approached to take a seat, and two of us stood while she was being seated.  The other two brokers remained in their chairs and nodded a "Hello" as we introduced ourselves around the table. In mere moments, the two who failed to stand were absolutely mortified when they discovered that the woman was our new branch manager.

## Solutions:
1. Sign up for a class on manners and etiquette training.
2. If you don't like the classroom setting, head for your nearest bookstore where you'll find shelves full of books on good manners.
3. Seek out a consultant who can walk you through the detailed niceties of meetings, introductions, dinners, and so forth.
4. Watch the seasoned professionals and learn from them. They're easy to spot in a crowd.
5. Make and keep a commitment regarding RSVPs.
6. Send timely handwritten thank-you notes.
7. Take pride in your socially correct behavior.

## Results:
1. Your newly refined manners will speak volumes about you as a professional who cares.
2. You'll receive infinite respect from your peers, bosses and spouse or potential spouse.
3. Clients and prospects will notice and be impressed with your social graces.
4. You'll be confident in your personal introductions.
5. You will feel more comfortable in professional settings.
6. You will never be intimidated by a competitor or client or prospect who demonstrates good manners.
7. Your RSVPs and thank-you notes will always be noticed.
8. You will be perceived as a professional.
9. You will be a star at impression management.

**P.S.** "The successful business person invests time and effort into managing the impression he or she gives others." – Theresa Thomas, business etiquette consultant

# REPUTATION

## How to Augment and Enhance Your Million-Dollar Reputation

*"The purest treasure mortal times afford is spotless reputation."*
*— William Shakespeare*

**Premise:**

You are never exactly as good or as bad as your reputation. Sometimes you get more pluses than you deserve, and vice versa. How your friends, associates, customers and prospects think and talk about you has a direct impact on your sales success or lack thereof. It can take years to build reputations of choice and one foolish act to destroy them.

Understand what a reputation can do for you or against you. Take time to decide the reputation that you desire. Realize that you have more than one reputation – as a friend, sales consultant, golfer, speaker, volunteer and parent. Carefully manage each of your reputations every day. Your reputation will precede you, and follow you, too!

**Symptoms of Impending Disaster:**

*   You have never seriously considered the power of a reputation.
*   You have never consciously worked at developing your desired reputations.
*   During your quarterly reviews, your sales manager tells you that the administrative team is disgusted with your sloppy client and prospect records.
*   Your sales manager points out that your teammates choose not to arrange role-playing sessions with you because you typically cancel at the last minute.
*   Your friends joke about the fact that you're always late for social functions.
*   At the end of the month, the order entry department team says, "Just wait; he'll arrive with a stack of orders at the last minute

and expect us to work overtime."

- When your sales manager calls on clients and prospects for reviews, they comment on how they like you, how you make excellent presentations, but you never follow up.

## Story:

Recently, my wife, a long-time designer, decided it was time to build our own home. In the process, we interviewed architects, builders and related consultants. When it got down to the final steps of choosing the ultimate builder, we interviewed three local, successful firms, each with an excellent image in our community. After our initial meetings, it was time to check references and confirm reputations.

While all three checked out in terms of quality of work and character, one stood out from a very special viewpoint. When I asked about Steve Cameron, the builder we ultimately selected, his reputation made the difference. You see, each of his prior clients said he showed up every day on schedule, did what he said he would do, and not only did he build under schedule, he also completed building under cost. Weighing in the references and the reputation story, it became very clear that, because of his reputation among prior clients, he would walk his talk and deliver. He got the contract. Incidentally, he built the home under time AND under cost. We couldn't be more pleased. The key part of our decision was his reputation, which he had built, one house at a time, one client at a time, over several years. To this day, he still calls to see if there's anything he needs to do to ensure that, as clients, we're still 100% satisfied.

## Solutions:

1. Look around and ask yourself, "What are the specific reputations of other successful people?"
2. Take stock of your own reputation by asking your friends, family and business associates. Get specific.

3. Write each of their above comments down.
4. Think about your desired reputations by role. What do you want them to be?
5. Write out each reputation on a piece of paper, i.e., the accounting department says that Jack's travel and expense report is always perfect.
6. Review your desired reputations each and every day. Visualize them.
7. Live by your chosen reputations. You will move toward that which you dwell upon.
8. In your business plan, your desired reputation should be the first item and it will set the tone for everything else.
9. Build an unique and memorable one-person brand.

**Results:**
1 People on your sales team will compliment you on specifics that relate to your new reputation.
2. You will no longer be the butt of the jokes in the office but, rather, the sales professional other team members revere.
3. Young sales rookies will come to you and say, "How did you do it?"
4. Your enhanced reputations will lead to additional opportunities.
5. When you're in a competitive battle for business, your reputation as a dependable sales professional who walks his talk, will always carry the day.
6. When the sales management team is electing someone for a critical assignment, your reputation will be the deciding factor as to whether or not you are selected.

**P.S.** Henry Ford, founder of the Ford Motor Company, once said, "You can't build a reputation on what you're going to do."

# COMMUNICATION

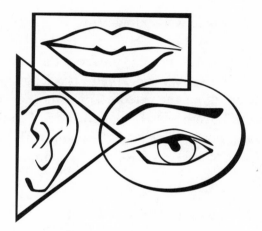

# PRESENCE

## It's Showtime!  Add Persuasive Power to Your Presentations

*"The best effect of fine persons is felt after we have left their presence."*
*— Ralph Waldo Emerson*

**Premise:**

When some people walk into a room, everybody knows they're present. They just stand out. They attract others because they have a presence about them – facial expression, the way they hold their head high, their dress, their style, their body language, and the way they walk, the air about the person. This is not a genetic or innate trait; anyone can learn how to be poised and feel distinguished and, as a result, stand out in a crowd.  The plain truth is: you have less than ten seconds to make a favorable first impression. One, two, three, four....

**Symptoms of Impending Disaster:**
- You consistently find yourself just fading into the crowd.
- There's nothing distinct about you, your dress, your actions or your communications.
- People often do not remember who you are or remember meeting you.
- You walk timidly into group meetings.
- You don't feel or act as if you are poised, confident.

**Story:**

Years ago, a friend and a partner of mine, Doug Wood, and I were in New York on business. Doug had developed a tremendous presence based on his successes, confidence and experience in business and as an actor. One evening, as we were approaching a very important meeting at a prestigious skyscraper in midtown Manhattan, Doug turned to me as we were entering the elevator and said, "Jack, when we walk out of this elevator and into that board room, we're going to act as if we own this entire building."

And that's exactly what we did. When the elevator opened, we walked in as if it were our personal elevator. As we entered the boardroom for the presentation, we stood tall and walked tall, and everyone in the room could feel, detect and smell our confidence. There was a definite air of strength in our presence.

## Solutions:

1.  Always stand tall. Why shouldn't you? Look at the alternative!
2.  Believe in yourself and your story.
3.  Feel radiant from within and you will be outwardly radiant.
4.  Smile and deliberately put a gleam in your eye.
5.  Feel as if you actually shine.
6.  Have a confident look in your eye.
7.  Pay attention to your dress. Make sure it's as sharp as the image you intend to convey.
8.  Say to yourself, "When I walk into the meeting room, everybody will notice me."
9.  Have a distinct style.
10. Exude confidence.

## Results:

1.  When you go to the dictionary and look up a definition for a true sales professional with presence – you will see your picture there.
2.  People will pay more attention to you because they sense your confidence and presence.
3.  Conversations will start to be directed to you and about you.
4.  You will be given extra credit for the air of presence about you.
5.  Your confidence will grow and so will your sales.
6.  People will want to do business with you.
7.  You will be like a magnet in terms of attracting attention and respect. This is charisma.

**P.S.** With your strong presence, you will get more mind space from your clients, prospects and peers.

# NONVERBAL

## Make Sure Your Walk Equals Your Talk

*"People buy based on their senses, and everything you can do to positively affect their senses can and will affect your abilities to sell to them."*
*— Robert C. Brenner*

**Premise:**

When you are in front of a client or prospect, your entire persona participates in the communication opportunity. You can't magically control the client and prospect into just hearing your words and ignoring your body language. The whole YOU talks to your client and prospect: eyes, arms, facial expressions, voice tones and posture. Great content delivered with conflicting body language is a recipe for confusion.

This is confirmed by a study conducted at UCLA by Dr. Albert Mehrabien, who found that only seven percent of human communication comes from the actual words spoken. The other 93% of any message is received by nonverbal communication – 38% from the speaker's voice and how the words are spoken, and the majority (55%) in the speaker's **body language**.

**Symptoms of Impending Disaster:**

- While asking for the order, your eyes are always looking away from the client or prospect.
- You are uncomfortable looking people in the eye.
- When at the client's office, you find yourself slumping in your chair.
- When you're walking down the street and see your reflection in a store window, you notice that you've been walking with your head down, shoulders hunched.
- When you look in the mirror, you don't see a confident, radiant sales professional.
- When answering objections, you sink down in your chair and look as if you were whipped.

**Story:**

OCS, Officer's Candidate School, was a competitive jungle. Your class ratings counted in your future career assignments. As a result, I observed closely how the leading candidates approached our teaching staff. They were confident, heads up, standing tall, nothing negative emanated from their bodies. Whether they aced the mission or took a big dose of constructive comments, they never lost their positive body language. And, when they led the class in a maneuver, the fellow officer candidates responded positively and immediately to their orders.

I also carefully observed officer candidates in the lower half of our class. It was obvious that their communications were conveyed with no conviction in their voices and, when they were aggressively challenged by the teaching staff on one of their leadership assignments, they would lower their heads and walk away with rejection stamped all over them.

**Solutions:**
1.  Be aware that your body and voice must be in sync.
2.  Observe other people's body communications.
3.  Analyze others who are confident, successful and have positive body language and also those who are unsuccessful.
4.  Prior to each call – even if over the phone – remind yourself to be aware of positive body communications.
5.  During your client and prospect calls, make sure your words match your body language.
6.  After each call, review what your body did as compared to what your mouth said.
7.  Watch how clients and prospects react to you when you sit up, lean forward and look them in the eye with a confident smile.
8.  Ask your sales manager to observe you in action and give you feedback regarding your nonverbal communications.

**Results:**
1. Because your "talk" is in sync with your "walk," clients and prospects will begin responding more favorably.
2. People will take you more seriously in all situations.
3. If your body radiates confidence, it will give your mental attitude an extra boost.
4. Because there is no conflict in communication between your body and your words, there will be no confusion over your true message.

**P.S.** "Your true intentions will always be most readily communicated through your body and tone of voice; and it's through these, more so than through any words you could possibly say, that people will decide if they like you, if they trust you, and if they want to do business with you." – Victoria Labalme

# ENTHUSIASM

## Your Enthusiasm Needs a Booster Shot

*"If you aren't fired with enthusiasm, you will be fired with enthusiasm."*
*— Vince Lombardi*

### Premise:

Clients and prospects will mirror your passion or lack of it. Why should they be enthusiastic if you aren't? Why should they be enthusiastic about a solution or opportunity if you're not? If you want action on the part of your clients and prospects, YOU should provide the emotional spark in the form of your personal passion. When you believe, they believe. Your passion for a product or service or position speaks volumes.

### Symptoms of Impending Disaster:

- You notice your presentations are registering "ZERO" on the client and prospect excitement meter.
- Boring, bland and unimaginative would describe your presentations.
- When you look in the mirror, you don't see a real spark in your eye.
- Your suggestions to clients and prospects come across as just matter-of-fact, with no compelling reasons to act.
- When you discuss new enhancements to your product or service, you give it a ho-hum "Just some more change in product development" approach.
- You look at enthusiastic people with suspicion.
- You think it's unprofessional to be enthusiastic. You see yourself as being reserved, under control, with no emotions – "Mr. Cool."
- You feel it's unprofessional to be passionate.

### Story:

Recently, while shopping at Staples for a new cell phone, I

encountered a young sales clerk who was persistently helpful. He had a barrel of enthusiasm to go with it – he was passionate. Staples didn't have the specific phone I wanted in stock, but he was so enthusiastic about their service and support that he would arrange to have it delivered to my home, or I could pick it up at another store in town. As I thanked him and started to leave, he walked up to me with that big smile again and told me about the new model his manager had just received in his office for display only. He was sure he could convince his manager to sell it to me today rather than hold it as a display. Again I started to leave and he said, "We want your business. Would you stay one more minute while I get an approval?"

How could I say "no?" Yes, his enthusiasm won the day and Staples got the order. I made a point of sending his manager a letter complimenting the young man.

## Solutions:
1. Prior to a call, decide how you can be enthusiastic with specific ideas with this client or prospect.
2. When new changes are announced, take the initiative. Be enthusiastic and passionate about the change.
3. When you hear your old bland sales message starting to become a canned formula, stop, reload and fire again with passion and enthusiasm.
4. Look people in the eye as you pass them and say, "Good morning, how are you today?" Be sure to add your big smile.
5. Enjoy catching yourself being passionate and enthusiastic. Relish it.

## Results:
1. You will discover that you have more energy.
2. You'll find your passion and enthusiasm are contagious. Your associates will begin to pick up on the enthusiasm, too.
3. People will not hesitate to share ideas with you because they know you won't rain on their parade.

4.  Your passion and enthusiasm will attract enthusiasm from your clients and prospects.
5.  With this newfound passion for your products and services, you will discover more and better client and prospect solutions.
6.  With passion and enthusiasm, you will melt many objections away.
7.  With your belief, passion and enthusiasm, more clients and prospects will also believe.

**P.S.** Every day, wear your passion and enthusiasm like a fine suit of new clothes.

# PRESENTATION

## It's Showtime! Add Persuasive Power to Your Presentations

*"Talking and eloquence are not the same:*
*To speak and speak well are two things."*
*— Ben Johnson*

**Premise:**

When in front of a client or prospect, it is showtime – lights, camera and action. When the film starts to roll, you want to be at the Academy Awards, winning the Oscar for the Best Actor. Don't waste a client or prospect's time or *your* time with poorly prepared and delivered presentations. That's the ultimate insult to your client and prospect. Show up early, ready to sing and dance; take advantage of the opportunity. Never be boring; choose to be memorable. At Gettysburg, Harvard professor Edward Everett spoke for two hours and no one recalls his message. Lincoln spoke only 10 sentences using 272 words in five minutes. His words will be remembered for eternity.

**Symptoms of Impending Disaster:**

- You tell the same old story over and over with the same clients and prospects.
- You're never asked to speak at the company meetings.
- You're obviously very nervous in your face-to-face client communications.
- Your presentations start with a weak, "Hi, I'm glad to be here."
- Your presentations are not organized and, instead, come off like random record selections.
- Your presentations ramble and are too long.
- Your presentations are one-way, with no client or prospect involvement.

- You start your presentations with one inflection, speed of delivery, and volume in your voice, and you never change any of these variables.
- You never have a client/prospect call to action in your presentations.

**Story:**

In 1995 at the Grand Hyatt in San Francisco, we were conducting a seminar for a group of financial planners. I asked one of our younger sales trainees, George, to step in with very little notice and do a presentation at the last moment. The truth came out quickly. He didn't know the presentation, he was nervous and he obviously hadn't practiced. He looked like a deer in headlights. I quickly stepped back in, and asked if I could clarify a few points.

The next day, the real work began. Now, let's be fair – it was partly my fault because I hadn't provided the right type of training for George in this area of his business. After a number of serious training sessions, his presentations started to shine because of his dedication. George went on to become an outstanding performer and an excellent speaker and is frequently asked to speak at large meetings today.

**Solutions:**

1. Ask for help from your sales management.
2. Join Toastmasters, get involved and speak as often as possible.
3. Seek help from a professional speaking coach.
4. Invest your money in tapes and books on public speaking.
5. Commit to practice regularly.
6. Get quality tape and video recorders and record yourself and, of course, then listen and watch yourself.
7. Seek constructive criticism.
8. Design a structure in your presentation – an opening, points of wisdom, close, and a call to action.
9. Use stories to make your point.

10. Learn to pause, use different speeds, and change the inflection of your voice.
11. Developing and delivering show-stopping presentations is a learned skill, requiring hours of practice.

**Results:**
1.  Your presentation skills will move up on the charts.
2.  Your confidence as a presenter will soar.
3.  You will connect with your clients and prospects.
4.  You will receive improved client and prospect response.
5.  You will have fewer follow-up requests because the clients will not have missed key information in your presentation.
6.  You will be asked to speak at big company events.
7.  The rookies will stand at your door for presentation tips.
8.  You will have a reputation as a fine presenter.

**P.S.** "Radio is theater of the mind and so is the telephone. Through voice mastery and descriptive speech, you can project images that are infinitely more vivid than anything captured by a camera. Weave colorful stories in great detail so your audience can "see" what you mean." – Susan Berkley, author of the best-seller *Speak to Influence*, on www.greatvoice.com.

# QUESTIONS

## Ask Questions or You Will Be Asked to Leave!

*"The important thing is not to stop questioning."*
*— Albert Einstein*

**Premise:**

The quality of the answers you receive is based on the quality of questions you ask. Do you really think your customers and prospects sit around waiting for you to appear in front of them? Are they saying, "I wish Jack would call on me again"? And, further, that when you do arrive, they immediately sit you down and tell you how to sell to them? The answer is a loud and unequivocal "NO!" Customers and prospects possess all the information you need to determine how you can help them. Only through applying the learned skill of asking sincere questions and then skillfully listening does the sales process begin and proceed forward. It's up to you to elicit that information subtly. Keep asking your clients and prospects sincere questions for the right reasons.

**Symptoms of Impending Disaster:**

- You ask for the order and you get "No" too many times because you've failed to uncover your client's and prospect's needs and objections.
- On call preparation, you note that you have not prepared any meaningful questions for your clients and prospects.
- You feel uncomfortable asking your clients and prospects questions.
- You don't feel the need to ask questions during a sales call.
- You feel that questions cause you to lose control of the conversation. Wrong. They help you gain control.
- You've never read books or listened to CD's on how to effectively use questioning in the sales process.
- You don't know the difference between an opening question and closing question.

## Story:

As a young boy, one of our sons, Wade, was bashful when it came to asking questions. Let's be fair – he was only 10 years old at the time. However, Judy and I wanted to encourage him to speak up and be heard. I took him on a trip with me to Washington, D.C., and while we were sitting in the hotel lobby one day, I asked him to ask the attendant at the front desk for directions to a restaurant where we had reservations for dinner. I told him I would wait for him in the lobby. After 15 minutes walking back-and-forth in front of the reception counter, Wade finally stepped forward and popped the question to the hotel receptionist. With our directions, we went to our dinner and now, 23 years later, he's a real pro at asking questions, finding the pain, getting solutions, and getting what he wants.

## Solutions:

1. Prepare written questions in advance for every single call.
2. Always ask a client or prospect if you can ask a few questions in order to get information that will determine how you can help them.
3. Practice asking your questions.
4. Use both closed and open-end questions. A closed question gives your prospect a simple choice: Yes or No. An open question gives the client or prospect room to answer in a variety of ways, for example: "Tell me, what is it you value about my competitor's products and services?"
5. Always use the "Why did you select my competitor?" question. (If that's the case).
6. In the sales process, always ask, "What is the next step?"
7. After each call, review your questions and the answers you received.

## Results:

1. With just a few, well-researched questions, you will now get better and more complete information.
2. As a result of questions, you will find better solutions for your

clients and prospects.

3. Your clients and prospects will now have increased respect for you because of your concern for their needs.
4. You will improve your sales-to-close ratio.
5. You will find yourself going down fewer dead-end streets.
6. Your management team will respect and appreciate your professional approach to finding client solutions.
7. Through questioning, you will uncover unstated objections.

**P.S.** Enjoy the art of asking questions, the pleasure of learning and the joy of sales success.

# LISTEN

## If You Don't Listen, Your Job Will Be Listed in the Classifieds

*"Opportunities are often missed because we are broadcasting when we should be listening." — Anonymous*

**Premise:**

As sales professionals, we assume we know how to listen effectively. Effective listening entails far more than turning on your ears. The fact is, listening successfully is a learned skill and few sales people ever have any education on the how and why of listening. Effective listening is a vital key to successful sales; you must find the client and/or prospect's pain and understand it. Prospects will tell you their needs if you ask questions and then listen seriously. There's no value if you ask questions and then just charge ahead without reaping the benefit of having really listened to the answers.

**Symptoms of Impending Disaster:**
- When reviewing your calls, sales managers consistently tell you that you missed key points of need cited by the customer or prospect.
- When you review your business sales statistics, you're faced with a low closing ratio. You weren't listening.
- Upon reflection, you realize you've talked far too much in sales calls.
- You can't wait to jump into a conversation because you're trying to talk and make your point. That's not listening.
- When the client and/or prospect gave you the buy signal, you didn't hear it and just kept right on rambling.

**Story:**

In 2002, we set out to build a new home in Indian Wells, CA. In the process, we interviewed and considered three very fine, highly recommended architects in our community. In the process, we gave them our written guidelines and the rationale behind these specific guidelines, many of which were from my wife, Judy, who is an accomplished interior designer.

After the interview, Architect #1 came to our home and presented his specific ideas without mentioning any of Judy's considerable input.

Architect #2 came calling and gave a polite and cursory nod to what Judy had outlined, saying, "I think we can use some of your ideas when we get into the drawing stage."

Architect #3 invited us to his office and asked us to visit some of his completed homes in the community. In the process, he reviewed all of Judy's comments and requests, and pointed out how he would include them in his original layout and design and wanted her professional input.

The envelope, please? Yes, Architect #3 – Michael Kiner – won the business. Judy and Michael designed a home that reflected our needs and desires. It pays to listen and use your client and prospect information.

Oh yes – we referred Michael to a personal friend and he is now designing a home for them. Yes, one plus one can equal three.

## Solutions:

1. Accept effective listening as a key component for a successful sales career.
2. Listen with your eyes as well as your ears.
3. Remember the rule of thumb: Talk one-third of the time, and listen two-thirds of the time.
4. Always take notes during a sales presentation.
5. Periodically repeat your client or prospect's comments and ask if you have cited them correctly. This validates their ideas and ensures harmony.
6. After each call, evaluate your listening performance. Give yourself an honest grade.
7. Ask your sales managers to observe your work and give you input regarding your listening ability.

## Results:

1.  You will find that you are receiving more pertinent information from your clients and prospects.
2.  You will waste less time and energy going down avenues that are dead ends.
3.  You will provide more effective solutions for your clients and prospects.
4.  Your clients and prospects will respect you more because you listened to them – you validated them.
5.  People will enjoy talking to you because you actively listen to them.
6.  You will experience much greater sales success.

**P.S.** Listen your way to sales success.

# MOTORMOUTH

## Don't Let Your Motor Mouth Drive You Off the Success Highway

*"When you compare the value of talking to listening, in a sales communication, it's not even a contest. Talking comes in last every time." – Jack Perry*

**Premise:**

Yes, we all fall in love with our own voices. It seems to fill the time and eliminate the need to get down to the true work of listening and extracting those gems that will lead you to the needs and wants of your customers and prospects, to find the real need. The star sales professional is infrequently the fastest mouth in the West. In essence, the real sales professionals shut up and listen – and their sales go up. Verbosity, on your part, will cost you sales and reputation.

**Symptoms of Impending Disaster:**

- You frequently notice that the client and prospect seem to lose interest in your communication.
- You're getting fewer and fewer questions from your clients and prospects.
- As the sales call starts, you immediately go to your speech mode rather than considering an exchange of information.
- Upon reviewing your notes from a sales call, you notice the client and prospect said very little, in fact, sometimes nothing at all.
- You can't stand silence during a sales call.
- You think you can just talk over any objection.
- You believe that by continuous talking, you will, in some magical way, answer all of their objections.
- In the weekly sales meetings, you always add your two cents' worth. Many times, that's exactly what it's worth.
- Clients and prospects have to interrupt you to ask questions.
- Frequently on your phone conversations, people will say, "Well, I have to go now."
- At social events, you dominate conversations with your endless flow of chatter.

**Story:**

As a young, green, life insurance salesman with Occidental Life, I had a Ph.D. in Motor Mouth. I loved to hear my voice and I hated to hear those sales-killing objections. While Len, my sales manager was making a call with me one day, he took me aside after the client presentation and said, "Jack, this is not a speech or a filibuster. It's not about you, it's about them. You are talking too much. You cannot learn when you're talking."

That wake-up call caused me to reverse the "I" and "YOU" ratio of conversation.

**Solutions:**

1. Set a communication goal of two-to-one. Allow clients and prospects to talk twice as much as you do.
2. Take notes in your calls and review afterwards that you, in fact, did not do all the talking.
3. Allow for silence in the conversation.
4. Ask others to observe you in your communications and give you timely and candid feedback.
5. Practice talking less in your social conversations. Avoid the temptation to one-up other people with your voice.
6. Use phrases like, "Tell me more, and why," and then be quiet. Listen.
7. Give your mouth a rest and learn a thing or two.

**Results:**

1. You will immediately receive more vital information from clients and prospects.
2. Your clients and prospects will feel good because you've given them the floor and allowed them to express their views.
3. Your presentations will change from a speech to a consultation.
4. You will experience increased sales by virtue of the information the client or prospect shares with you.
5. You will have more friends.

**P.S.** "Talk is cheap because supply exceeds demand." – Anonymous

# OBJECTIONS

### Don't Object to Objections: Use Them as a Superhighway to Closing Sales

*"If you can't confidently and successfully handle objections, you're an amateur in the sales game and will get paid as an amateur."*
*— Jack Perry*

**Premise:**

In the process of finding the client or prospect's needs and then offering solutions, you will encounter resistance or objections. Remember, no objection equals no real sale. You're just an order-taker in the right place at the right time. When you're an order-taker, you're just lucky, but luck is not a skill you can count on to put money in your bank account consistently.

Objections are questions in disguise. Learn how to deal successfully with objections and you can always count on increased sales with your clients and prospects.

**Symptoms of Impending Disaster:**

- You don't have a written list of all the possible objections you might encounter.
- You don't prepare for objections by role-playing and practicing your answers.
- You actually fear objections.
- When clients or prospects object, you typically agree with them, just to keep the peace.
- You lose too many sales and don't know the reason why.
- When clients and prospects object, you don't acknowledge their objection. You just try to talk over them, or past it.

**Story:**

While making calls with one of my sales team members one day, I watched Bob get into an argument with a prospect. It seemed that the prospect didn't care for Bob's product and Bob chose to argue the merits of the product rather than probe for the reasons why the prospect didn't see the value of his product. Not only did he lose the debate, he wasted valuable time and didn't get the sale. In the end, both the prospect and the sales person lost time and energy and Bob went away empty-handed. It would have been better to agree to disagree and move on.

**Solutions:**

1. Understand that an objection is really a question in disguise. "Your price is too high" really means, "Why is your price so high?"
2. Always have a list of all the objections you might encounter.
3. Practice answering objections in a role-play format.
4. Ask for input from your sales management team and have them observe you in action.
5. Anticipate and seek objection. Actually ask the client or prospect if they have any objections.
6. Know how to reposition the objection in the client and prospect's mind with a positive benefit.
7. When presented with an objection, consider using the "feel," "felt" and "found" approach.
8. Your mantra should be: "I loooooove objections."
9. Invest in a copy of the Questions workbook offered through Selling Power Magazine and Dr. Donald Moine, the author of *Unlimited Selling Power*.

**Results:**

1. You will be confident in all of your sales calls because you are prepared for objections.
2. You will uncover the true objections.
3. There will be no mystery as to where you are in the sales process.
4. You will have fewer dead-end sales calls. There won't be a lot of time, effort and energy wasted and a lost sale because you didn't uncover and answer the objection.
5. Your sales closing ratio will go up.

6. You will have the opportunity to enjoy increased sales and income.

**P.S.** When you are prepared to answer objections, then objections become your new best friend.

# CLOSING

## Insure Your Success by Asking for the Business

*"Timid sales consultants have skinny children."*
*– Tyler Carr*

### Premise:

Sales happen when you find the prospect's or client's pain, provide the solution and ask the client/prospect to approve the solution. In sales, we call this The Order. If you don't continue to advance or close the sale by asking for the order, you were just having a conversation. A conversation might be pleasant and could even be a good time-filler, but it doesn't help the client or prospect, your company or you. Remember, a client or prospect truly expects you to ask for the order and help them make a decision. "The secret to selling ... It's always in the asking," – Bill Brooks. If you never ask, the answer will always be "No."

### Symptoms of Impeding Disaster:
* You're afraid to ask the big question: "Shall we get started? Will you approve the order?"
* You have low sales numbers compared to the number of pre-sentations you make.
* When you review your client and prospect account status, you find you have far too many clients or prospects just "thinking it over."
* You find that you truly take rejection personally, and thus, avoid it. If you don't ask, you can't be rejected, can you?
* You don't practice asking for the order by role-playing with your sales peers or sales managers.
* Your sales numbers are alarmingly low.

### Story:

Bob Cassato was the number one salesman for his company for many years. The company moved him to its worst territory. After three months he was number one again. Tom, the sales manager, called him and asked him his secret for success. Bob said it was nothing special. The next month Bob was on top of the leader board. Again, Tom called Bob to ask him his secret. Again, Bob said he did nothing special. After leading a third month in a row, Tom couldn't contain his curiosity regarding the Cassato success formula. He made a special trip to spend time with Bob. At dinner, Tom said, "We gave you the worst territory and within three months you are leading this company. What is your secret?"

Bob said, "You know that six-page sales brochure the company put out? I simply go to page one, read it to the prospect, then ask the prospect to buy, then I read page two to the prospect, ask him to buy, then page three, four, five and six asking him to buy at the end of each page." Tom then asked, "What if the prospect doesn't buy after page six?" Bob said, "I go back to page one, read it, then ask him to buy." Moral of the story: Salesmen don't close enough. Bob went on to become the national sales manager and then CEO of a major financial services firm.

## Solutions:
1. Understand that asking for the order is just part of the business.
2. Write out your closing questions.
3. Role-play with a sales manager or team member constantly to maintain your edge.
4. Ask your sales manager to come with you and observe your actions and conversations.
5. Keep records on closing questions and results and, most importantly, be honest with yourself.

## Results:
1. You'll feel more confident.
2. You'll have fewer clients or prospects in the "I want to think it over" category.
3. You'll find the real objections and have the opportunity to answer them.
4. You know that every "No" you receive gets you closer to a "Yes."
5. You will have increased respect from your peers and sales

management team.
6.   Your sales will move upward.

**P.S.** "Ask and you shall receive." – John 16:24

# TEMPER

## Are Your Temper Tantrums Totaling Your Career?

*"The things I never say never get me into trouble."*
*— Calvin Coolidge*

**Premise:**

Emotional control is expected from a sales professional. There's no place in the sales profession for temper tantrums when things don't go your way. If you can't control your emotions, how can you control the sales process? Yes, sales might be a contact sport, but you must channel your emotions and energies in a positive direction.

**Symptoms of Impending Disaster:**

- One day, you're emotionally up and the next day you're an emotional wreck.
- You allow small issues to upset you.
- You frequently just fire away at a client or team member for what others consider to be small or insignificant comments.
- Your fellow sales team members do not know how to read your emotions and, therefore, don't know how to approach you or rely upon you for input.
- You periodically argue with customers and prospects.
- You find yourself frequently raising your voice during family discussions.
- The sales management team doesn't give you big and demanding prospects, due to the fear that your temper might erupt.

**Story:**

In the early 1960s at IBM, Roy, our divisional executive vice president, could throw a public tantrum on a 10-second notice. He would virtually explode if things didn't go his way. In the short run and in the interest of our long-term success, we all hunkered down and took it on the nose. I can remember being so frustrated with

Roy's temper blasts that one day, in Kansas City, I wanted to jump out of a window in an eight-story building to escape the man.

Then, one Monday morning at our 7 a.m. meeting, his boss – the divisional president – unexpectedly slipped unnoticed into the back of the room. Right on cue, our manager exploded on a rookie who made a sub-par presentation. Then the real explosion took place. The divisional president asked to see Roy in a private office for a personal conversation. That was the last time I experienced Roy's temper.

### Solutions:

1. When you feel the temper start to fire up, count to 10 silently.
2. If you slip and let your temper fly, apologize.
3. Role-play with your sales management team, who will purposely put you on the spot or act combatively.
4. Get it out of your system: employ gross physical impact – pound the seat of your car, take up kickboxing, or do whatever it takes to get it out of your system without harming other living entities. Consider having a punching bag at your back door to use before entering your home each evening. Take out your frustrations and drain your temper on the bag and, as a result, you won't take it out on your friends and family.
5. Leave your temper at home or stay at home.

### Results:

1. You will have fewer arguments with your clients and prospects.
2. You will have more energy for positive action.
3. You will like yourself better.
4. You will receive help from your team members who were previously afraid to approach you because of your volatility.
5. Your personal life will be better.

**P.S.** Steady as she goes.

# PERSONAL GROWTH

# COACHABLE

## "Not Coachable" Often Means "Not Successful"

*"If you're not coachable, you'll soon be on the sidelines and ultimately in the grandstand as a spectator eating popcorn." — Jack Perry*

**Premise:**

All the great performers value coaching: actors who win Oscars, athletes who win MVP awards and politicians who are elected to their chosen office. No matter what you think, you CANNOT see yourself as others see you. You just can't be completely objective when it comes to YOU. Great sales professionals invest in coaches because they've chosen to maximize the return on their commitment and time investment as they pursue tapping into their true potential. Sales managers very quickly discern who is coachable within their team. Sales managers invest when their teammates invest. The coachable sales professionals receive more in company resources and time investment by the sales management team. Wouldn't you prefer this advantage?

**Symptoms of Impending Disaster:**
- You wouldn't think of asking for advice or coaching and are often considered a lone wolf. You even take pride in being "The Loner."
- You think people who invest their own money in a professional coach are just throwing their money down the drain.
- You staunchly defend your own way of doing things, regardless of the fact that your sales activity and sales performance aren't where they should be.
- When you receive advice in coaching from your sales management team, you give them one of the following responses:
  a. You verbally agree with your sales manager's advice that you need to implement for increased sales success, but then you continue doing things the same old way.

b.   When you receive sales advice from your sales manager, you quickly react with a "Yes, but ..."

## Story:

Recently, I was speaking with Dottie Walters, President of Walters International Speakers Bureau and author of the best-selling book on speaking, *Speak and Grow Rich*. Dottie and I were discussing the "Do's" and "Don'ts" of successful speakers and that reminded me of a survey taken of the National Speakers Association members.

When the top speakers were surveyed and asked what they would have done differently, above anything else they indicated that they would have invested in a coach earlier in the game. They would have invested in themselves by bringing in a proven expert rather than insisting on traveling the ups and downs of the speaker learning curve alone. They would not just rely on Lady Luck and time.

## Solutions:

1. Be proactive. Seek out coaching.
2. If you discover you have negative thoughts about having a personal coach, immediately replace that thought with the positive opportunities that come with professional coaching.
3. Ask others for advice regarding specific areas you could improve.
4. Investigate professional coaches who are available.
5. Make notes when you receive coaching, and then repeat it to the coach to ensure you have it right.
6. Schedule your coaching instruction for immediate implementation in the days and weeks ahead, and make yourself keep that appointment with your better future.
7. Seek out success stories from coaches and your peers about sales coaching experiences.
8. Offer to coach some of the new, less experienced members of your team. Teaching will reinforce your skills.

**Results:**

1. You will quickly see and eliminate poor sales habits, replacing them with successful habits used by winners that will immediately improve your sales results.
2. You will experience greater personal satisfaction as your skills improve.
3. Your potential will be fully utilized.
4. Others will seek you out for advice.
5. Others' successes and failures will be lessons for you.
6. You will have more sales success for the same invested effort.
7. As you now coach others you will, in the process, reinforce your own new skills.
8. With improved skills, your overall competence will increase.
9. You will be more effective in leading your clients and prospects to better decisions for increased profits.

**P.S.** Accelerate your sales success with a commitment to a coaching relationship.

# SELF-DEVELOPMENT

## The Best Investment You Will Ever Make is an Investment in Yourself

*"Education's purpose is to replace an empty mind with an open one."*
*– Malcolm Forbes*

**Premise:**

You have choices every day as to where to invest time, energy, resources, and your money. Without a doubt, you yourself are the single best asset in terms of where you should be investing your time and money. If you don't choose to invest in yourself, why should anyone else? Strong sales professionals don't expect their company to provide all their current and future education for success. Instead, they personally budget and invest meaningful dollars of their own for personal development.

**Symptoms of Pending Disaster:**

- Lately, your investment in yourself looks like the stock market on a bad day – falling off a steep cliff.
- You think it's the company's responsibility to pay for your sales education.
- You choose not to invest in educational experiences via books, tapes, CDs or classes.
- You don't have a professional library of resources in your home or office.
- Your skill level is actually level.
- You're doing nothing to sharpen your axe.

**Story:**

In the mid 1960s, when I left IBM and joined the financial services industry, I found that my new chosen industry didn't provide the same kind of forced education that "Big Blue" constantly put on you. One day, one of my clients came into the branch office and asked me, "What is it that you really do, Jack?" I have forgotten my answer but, to this day, I certainly remember his reply: "No, Jack. I disagree. You are a knowledge broker." I said, "Let's talk."

At our conversation's conclusion, I realized that I was, in fact, a "knowledge broker" and needed to pursue that path more effectively. From that point, I became someone who searched for pertinent knowledge and resources that I thought were important for my clients and prospects, and then shared it with them as part of my value-added service.

I further realized that, if I wanted to truly have that reputation, I would need to invest significantly in my own ongoing education. Down to the bookstore I trotted and out with the credit card, so that I could fill my shelves with books and tapes for my own development. Personal self-development has since been a significant part of my business success, personal growth and satisfaction.

### Solutions:
1. Sign up for publications that offer quick and concise reviews of the latest business books so that you know what you should be reading. Then, march yourself to a bookstore.
2. Enroll in a class. Take a weekend conference. Not only will it open your mind, it will have you associating and sharing energy with people who are growing.
3. Look to your future. Where can you be investing in yourself that will also benefit peers, community or your own family members?
4. Continually build a knowledge base.
5. Let your friends, clients and prospects know that you're on the hunt to invest in new educative opportunities for your expanded growth.

### Results:
1. You will have a reputation as a serious sales professional who

chooses to improve his or her skills.

2.  Rookies will come to you for advice.
3.  With your increased knowledge and skills, the sales managing team will come to you for increased advice and input.
4.  As your knowledge and skills increase, you will become a master of the sales process.
5.  Your confidence will soar.
6.  You have the knowledge and skills to separate yourself from the competition.

**P.S.** Hit the books and move past your competition. The best long-term sales professionals are constantly self-improvers.

# CRITICISM

## Turn Constructive Criticism from Your Enemy into Your Friend

*"He only profits from praise who values criticism."*
*— Christian Johann Heinrich Heine*

**Premise:**

No matter how many people tell us we're a "born natural" at sales, we do not emerge from the womb with all the knowledge and experience needed for sales success. An education, practice and exposure will help you grow and develop, but you are never objective when it comes to your own faults and needs for improvement. You need to see things as they really are. That's why it's so important to be open and amenable to constructive criticism. When constructive criticism is delivered on a timely basis, you have the opportunity to make immediate course corrections to reach your target more quickly. If you can't take constructive criticism, do yourself a favor – take yourself out of the sales game.

**Symptoms of Impending Disaster:**
- When somebody offers you constructive criticism, your mind slams shut like a prison door.
- You flat-out resent constructive criticism.
- You dislike any sales manager who gives you constructive criticism and, instead, take it as a personal attack.
- When your peers offer advice, you think they've overstepped their boundaries with you.
- You look at your firm's appraisal system as a waste of time and not a valuable tool for personal growth.
- Clients and prospects offer constructive criticism and you shut them down.

**Story:**

In the spring of 1967, I was given the opportunity to turn

around and rebuild the Los Angeles office of what is now Smith Barney. Believing that the #1 asset in any business is your people, I implemented a personal review system that I had utilized during my IBM management opportunities. In the rehab process of my L.A. office, I recognized that one of my team members, Mike, had tremendous potential as a personal money manager for his clients. But he seemed to lack the necessary energy; he needed to get into better physical condition. We had The Conversation.

Granted, this kind of advice would be taken personally but my advice stood soundly on my observations. My sole objective was to help him realize his potential.

Just a few months ago, Mike told me about his reaction to that advice some forty years ago. On his way home from the office, he was so angry over my suggestions during the personal review that he had to pull his car off the freeway and collect himself. "Who does Jack think he is, telling me...???" Then he said the light came on. "I realized that Jack cared enough about me and my future to tell me the truth." Mike quickly worked himself into fighting shape, took up golf and started toward success.

Mike is now physically fit, a single-digit handicap golfer and a successful money manager for his many wealthy clients. To this day, Mike is highly selective and has to turn business away.

## Solutions:

1. Tell yourself every morning that you have an open mind to constructive criticism and consciously practice that thinking throughout the day.
2. Ask for constructive comments on a timely basis.
3. Send your ego on a long vacation with a one-way ticket.
4. When advice comes your way, pause just a moment to remind yourself that you have an open mind and an opportunity to learn and grow.
5. Thank people who took the time and effort for their input to your success.
6. Make notes as they offer their advice. This action on your part

nonverbally conveys respect for the person speaking to you.

7. As appropriate, implement the advice you receive.

**Results:**

1. With your open-armed reception of constructive ideas, you have removed a major obstacle from your future success.
2. You will have the opportunity to better utilize your time and resources.
3. You will receive valuable input for improving your sales skills and adapting to profitable habits.
4. Through being more coachable, you will experience rapid personal growth.
5. Clients and prospects will now take the time and effort to offer constructive criticism.

**P.S.** Use constructive criticism as a creative force. Make it work for you.

# ACCOUNTABILITY

## How Your Accountability Can Add to Your Bank Account

*"He that is good for making excuses is seldom good
for anything else." – Benjamin Franklin*

**Premise:**

Accountability is a proven trademark of dependable sales professionals. To win in the game of life, business and sales, you must be personally responsible for your actions as well as your non-actions. Only when you are accountable to yourself and then to others are you on the road to an improved performance. To become a successful sales professional you must be brutally honest with yourself. No rationalizations or excuses.

**Symptoms of Impending Disaster:**

- Deep down, you know you really don't like to face the facts.
- You're playing games with your time and personal accountability for sales and projects.
- When it comes to accountability and your sales quota, you're long on excuses.
- You don't volunteer to be responsible for special projects.
- You find you're having fewer important tasks assigned to you.
- Inwardly, you resist reporting the results of your sales activity for public view.
- You know you don't have current and accurate records for your client and prospect activity.

**Story:**

In the beautiful Ojai valley of Southern California, there is a private high school that teaches accountability in an unique way. Each student must have and properly care for a horse. It seems that there's something about the outside of a horse that's good for the inside of a person – accountability and responsibility. When you know that a living thing is completely dependent on you for survival, food, water and care, your sense of accountability steps up and takes priority over all your personal and unrelated "want-to's" and "rather-do's".

## Solutions:
1. Start with this fact: There are no excuses. Period.
2. Accept that you are the person responsible. End of subject.
3. Maintain up-to-date and accurate sales and activity records.
4. On a timely basis, measure yourself against your own standards and then adjust accordingly.
5. Ask team members and the sales management team to hold you accountable.
6. Be aware of others' accountability failures and learn from their errors.

## Results:
1. When you look in the mirror, you will like and respect yourself.
2. You'll no longer be wasting your time and emotion on your lame excuses.
3. You will have more time, energy and resources to produce positive results.
4. You'll see increased respect from your team members and your sales management team.
5. Your accountability will positively impact all of your clients' and prospects' actions.
6. You will be awarded the opportunity for increased responsibilities.
7. Your clients and prospects will know that they can count on you to perform.

**P.S.** We all prefer dealing with business professionals who demonstrate personal accountability.

# HABITS

## How to Free Yourself from the Hold of Undesirable Habits

*"Winning is not a sometime thing; it's an all-time thing. You don't win once in a while, you don't do things right once in a while, you do them right all the time. Winning is habit. Unfortunately, so is losing."*
*— Vince Lombardi*

**Premise:**

When it comes to choosing a potential mate, many a mother has told her daughter, "Don't marry him with a notion that you can change any of his habits that you don't like." You can't expect to change anyone's habits; it's hard enough trying to shift and control your own habits.

Your entire life direction is influenced by the habits you choose. While you can introduce new habits into your life and ditch the habits that don't favor you, it takes conscious time and effort to first realize what you need to stop doing and then implement the new habits of your choice. Of course, you must periodically check up to ensure your habits are truly habits and not an occasional convenient change.

**Symptoms of Impending Disaster:**

- You never put your own personal habits under the microscope for a personal examination.
- You've never studied the habits of winners. All of the following are examples of bad habits:
  a. You're habitually late for everything – meetings, phone appointments, projects, lunches and activity reports.
  b. You seem to overeat regularly.
  c. You never get up on time, and you're always going to bed later than you'd like.
  d. You never exercise.
  e. You constantly interrupt clients and prospects.

f.  You watch mindless TV.
g.  Your car is always dirty.
h.  You don't probe to find the real objections.
i.  You regularly miss your sales activity targets.
k.  Your New Year's Resolutions last until midnight New Year's Day.
l.  You have a habit of not developing good habits.
m.  You are easily distracted and not focused.

**Story:**

As a young IBM sales representative in the 1960s in Los Angeles, I was nervous and sought out one of the true professionals for direction. David was one of the real leaders in the office and he seemed to work and succeed like a machine. I asked him his real secret.

He said, "Jack, I realize that I'm competing with significant talent on the IBM team, and therefore, to use my resources to the utmost, I have to make sure I have specific habits that I put to use consistently every day. I run at 5:00 a.m. I eat a nutritious breakfast at 6:30 a.m., and I'm in the office at 7:30 a.m. And, I make 10 cold calls every day. I don't go home until I've completed those calls."

David walked his talk. He had many other healthy, ingrained habits that I'd seen him use repeatedly, day in and day out. He made it very clear to me that I first needed to get specific about what my habits would be, and then repeat these fundamental habits over and over without exception.

The best habit I took from David? Start early every day – without exception – and always do the most demanding task first. From there, it's all downhill.

**Solutions:**

1.  Take a hard look at the habits of two groups of sales people from your team and also from other organizations.
    a.  Failing or marginal producers.
    b.  Successful – top 10-20%.

2. List the habits of each group as you see them.
3. Now compare the salespeople's habits, side-by-side.
4. Notice the similar habits for each group.
5. Look around your life and list the habits of those you admire.
6. Ask leading sales consultants what their best habits are.
7. Take stock of your own habits that positively and negatively impact your sales success. Be tough on yourself.
8. It's decision time:
   a. Choose the habits you are going to bury, the bad guys.
   b. Choose the habits you are going to establish as controlling forces in your sales career, the good guys.
9. Monitor your chosen habits and keep them in force.
10. You can successfully create permanent new habits in 30-60 days.
11. You have now eliminated any mystery regarding why some sales consultants succeed and why some fail. It's habit.

**Results:**
1. You will experience the great habit exchange:
   a. Elimination of the destructive habits that torpedo your sales efforts.
   b. Added positive habits used by successful sales consultants.
2. Your whole life will change with your new, controlling habits.
3. You will get the results associated with your controlling habits:
   a. Exercise and nutrition habits give you more energy for all areas of your life.
   b. Being punctual brings new respect and opportunities.
   c. Meeting sales activity goals rewards you with increased sales and income opportunities.
4. Your habits of choice will lead you toward your desired results.
5. By employing the same habits used by successful sales consultants, you will have the opportunity to experience their types of success.

**P.S.** Habits are a controlling force of your life. Make them good ones. "Habits are stronger than reason." – George Santayana

# FOCUS

## With a Clear Focus, You Will Unleash Your Full Powers

*"When I look into the future, it's so bright it burns my eyes."*
*— Oprah Winfrey*

**Premise:**

Take a toy magnifying glass out on a sunny day and direct the sun's beams to a piece of paper below. What happens? Presto! Fire combusts because of focused energy. If you can do that with a toy magnifying glass, imagine what you can accomplish when you focus your talents, energies and resources on a specific opportunity. Remember, you must always be focused: focused on avoiding unworthy goals, or moving toward your chosen, focused goals.

**Symptoms of Impending Disaster:**

- Your "super-priority" projects number like quills on a porcupine's back.
- You're easily distracted by each new piece of paper, phone calls from clients/prospects or someone else talking in your ear.
- Your desk is a first-class mess.
- Nothing in your business plan is getting your full attention and, therefore, your best result simply isn't there.
- Your definition of focus is, "How many things can I do at once?"
- You allow your clients and prospects to change your focus each and every day.

**Story:**

A friend of mine was a consultant making trips frequently across the country to major corporations. I watched his closing ratio sag and the number of his engagements dramatically drop. He asked for some advice and, upon reviewing his business model, I noticed that he listed 10 different specialties. I said, "Sam – wow! How can you possibly be an expert on 10 things?"

It became very clear that Sam was trying to be all things to all people and he needed to define his true point of difference more thoroughly and clearly. Sam cleaned house and took on one strong point of difference as a consultant (managing change), became an expert – and has gone on to be a big success.

## Solutions:

1. Take out a piece of paper and list your sales projects.
2. Immediately throw out those that don't contribute to your goals.
3. Review your projects and rank them in priority from high to low.
4. Attack the highest priority project first and work at it until it is complete before moving on.
5. Make a point of physically checking off completed projects. This is a reward and will make you feel good while helping you move forward.
6. Focus the majority of your energy and resources on solutions.

## Results:

1. You will reduce your frustrations because you will have fewer distractions, both in front of you and in your mind.
2. You'll have the satisfaction of completing important projects.
3. By experiencing your success with the power of focus, you will concentrate on being even more focused.
4. Your associates won't bother you with minor requests because of your laser-like focus.
5. You'll begin to notice an increase in your success because of an eagle-eye focus rather than a disheveled approach across several projects.
6. By experiencing your success with the power of focus, you will concentrate at being even more focused.
7. Those important sales projects will be completed on a timely

basis and more sales will come your way.

**P.S.** Great golfers are coached to take dead aim when they putt for the dough. Great sales professionals also take dead aim at their sales targets and go for the dough.

# DISCIPLINE

## How to Become a Disciple of Discipline

*"Self-respect is the fruit of discipline. A sense of dignity grows with the ability to say "no" to one's self. — Abraham J. Hershel*

**Premise:**

You gain and maintain control of yourself by mastering discipline. Each day, you are confronted with hundreds of decisions and choices in all areas of your life – diet, exercise, study, personal development, work habits, the number of sales appointments you make and more. You can mold your habits with discipline, thereby focusing your talents and ideas and bringing your dreams to reality.

**Symptoms of Impending Disaster**

- You join the local fitness center, start with a trainer, set goals and then promptly quit in the first 90 days.
- You make a decision to change your diet – you read, study and start a new eating program and, in a few days, you're sneaking donuts at the local deli.
- You agree to role-play with one of your sales team members and then promptly quit after two sessions.
- You make a decision to read for an hour each morning before you attack your sales opportunities each day, but after a few mornings, you're back to sleeping in.
- You've decided that gossip is counterproductive and yet you can't help yourself.
- At the beginning of the year, you make a commitment to save an additional 10% toward your retirement. Instead, you start buying more things and the 10% is gone.
- You've decided to limit interruptions during your day, and yet you still let every possible phone call and event distract your sales process.

**Story:**

In the mid 1960s, I was a stockbroker in Newport Beach, California, for a company which is now Smith Barney. Growing up in an agricultural community, my Dad always forced me out of bed to start chores early; I was destined to enter the office early every morning. One day, I decided I'd like to be first in the office and gain the reputation as such. Another broker, Lou, had held that position for years by opening the office at 6:30 a.m.

The next morning, I came in at 6:15 a.m., rather than the usual 6:30, and when Lou arrived, he looked a little surprised, but didn't say a word. The next morning, when I arrived at 6:15 a.m., guess what? Lou was sitting in his office. This male-ego oriented dance continued until 5:15 a.m., when Lou and I declared a truce and agreed that we would both arrive at 6:30 a.m. Our respective discipline stayed intact and we shared the honor of being the first broker in the office each day.

**Solutions:**
1.  Choose the specific areas of your life where you want to exercise better discipline. Write these down.
2.  Don't include an item on this list unless it's absolutely important to you and you know you must follow through.
3.  Reward yourself each week as you exercise discipline in achieving these items.
4.  When you have a conflict over maintaining one of your disciplines, stop yourself and review the benefits as to why you established this particular discipline.
5.  Ask for a periodic accountability review from your sales manager.

**Results:**
1.  You'll experience better personal results in all aspects of your life.
2.  You will be more focused and less scattered.
3.  Through discipline, you will accomplish more of your chosen activities and goals.

4.  You won't have to look at a stack of unfinished items because –
    through discipline – you'll be on track.
5.  Your reliability meter will shoot up.

**P.S.** Use your discipline as the perfect tool for your self-mastery.

# PRACTICE

## How to Practice Perfectly to Enjoy a Perfect Performance

*"The work is in the practice – the fun is in the performance."*
*– Michael Caine*

**Premise:**

Making a sale puts food on the table, but perfecting your sales skill will make you rich. Practice does NOT make perfect. When you practice, you create consistency. Bad practice equals bad performance and, therefore, perfect practice DOES prepare you for a perfect performance.

Athletes committed to a sport retain coaches and practice with a specific purpose. Skills are developed on the practice field. Unfortunately, after graduating from a firm's sales training class, most sales people never again practice their presentations, work on answering objections or spend time asking questions. Instead, they mistakenly believe they've been "branded" and their skills will remain with them permanently without any cultivation until called into action.

**Symptoms of Impending Disaster:**

- You don't ask for constructive criticism about your selling skills.
- You find yourself giving the same presentation over and over without any improvement.
- When you plan your week and month's activity, no time is set aside to practice questions, objections, presentations and answering objections.
- In sales calls you find yourself fumbling with objections because you haven't practiced using them to your advantage.
- You're not cited as the poster child for having practiced and perfected your selling skills.
- You hurriedly review your client literature and brochures prior to client meetings because you haven't practiced for the presentation.

- You think practice is just for the rookies.
- When asked if you practice, you quickly reply, "I don't need to practice because I have experience, and it comes naturally to me."
- Your client and prospect questions are answered with a dangerous ad-lib.
- Sometimes you lose your place in your presentations.

**Story:**

Many years ago at a National Speakers Association meeting in Orlando, Florida, I had the opportunity to be in a session with Zig Ziglar after one of his memorable presentations. It was spellbinding. Zig magically used pauses, inflection in his voice, changes of speed and pace. It was a "100" on a "1 to 10" scale. During a question-and-answer session, when Zig was asked about practicing presentations, he commented that, while he'd given the presentation he'd presented that day at least a hundred times, he still practices it several hours on the day prior to the presentation.

**Solutions:**

1. Start with the image of a professional athlete. Professionals practice.
2. Establish non-selling times on your calendar to review and practice your sales skills.
3. Practice with a mind for improvement. Look for better ways.
4. Only perfect practice makes perfect performance.
5. Offer to role-play and ask others to help you with their candid comments.

**Results:**

1. We all remember taking a test and saying we aced it. Why? Because we were prepared. The same applies when you have practiced your business-selling skills.
2. With the knowledge that you are prepared, you'll have confidence, ask questions and deliver your presentation;

your confidence will soar.

3. Clients and prospects will respect your skillful delivery in answering objections, asking questions and presenting a solution.
4. You will quickly come across as a true sales professional.
5. You can now focus on your implementation of the sales process because you know that your selling skills are in top form.
6. You will be asked to speak at the big company meetings.
7. The rookies will knock on your door and ask for help.
8. You will land your points more effectively.
9. You will win some business in a close call just because of your competition's poorer selling skills and lack of preparation.

**P.S.** As an athlete, you will predictably play the way you practice. In the sales arena, when you practice with an eye toward perfection, you will predictably deliver your presentations, ask questions and answer objections in a professional manner.

# COASTING
## Turn Your Downhill Coasting into Mountain Climbing

*"The dedicated pursuit of your future dreams comes at the expense of your present comfort..." — Buzz Aldrin, second man on the Moon*

**Premise:**

When you coast as a sales professional, you never test yourself. You don't know what you really could achieve in the sales world. Most people want to reach a destination without first taking the trip; they don't want to pay the price to get there. Sure, I'd like to have abs like Mr. America, but I don't want to invest the hours and pain at the gym. Taking the course of least resistance is common for the average sales person. Remember, as a sales professional, you can only coast in one direction: Down and down and down. When you coast, the world will race past you.

**Symptoms of Impending Disaster:**
- You're selling just enough to keep your sales manager off your back, and that's good enough.
- You choose not to see the value of extra effort in exchange for extra results.
- Typically, you find yourself seeking the comfortable solution rather than investing the time, energy and resources to get better sales results.
- You're always prepared to start tomorrow. Of course, tomorrow never comes.
- Just like your New Year's Eve resolutions, you always make big plans and big promises at the end of the year, or at the end of the quarter.
- You always wonder why other people seem to get the opportunities that don't come your way.
- As you examine your investments, you find that you've invested zero dollars in yourself for your personal development and growth.

- After a big sales month, you start to relax, waste time, take your foot off the accelerator and coast.

## Story:

Life was really good for our younger son, Matt. A product of the sunny beaches of Laguna, California, this 22-year-old held a college degree, lived in some fine bachelor's digs and had an NCAA championship ring for UCLA volleyball to his credit.

With idealism as his bulwark, he embarked on the professional beach volleyball circuit but soon decided it wasn't for him. This wasn't providing him with the satisfaction that he needed. A year's stint as a bartender brought the funds for a long-dreamed-of surfing trek to exotic waters. Now what?

He looked around and realized that he was coasting on the Laguna Beach coast; life was quietly slipping by every day. His pals were taking serious jobs and starting careers. He was losing ground. One thing he knew: he had a passion for homes, architecture and real estate investments. He jumped into the real estate business and went the extra distance by quickly securing his broker's license. Recognizing the need to build his own business, he selected an area to farm. He tirelessly cultivated that area, knocking on doors, introducing himself and asking for the homeowners' time and interest. His business soon grew and he was knighted by an associate to share listings and sales. He got out of the coasting business and into the get-serious shoe leather business.

## Solutions:

1. Make a commitment to push yourself to new, higher standards in activity and sales.
2. Observe others around you enjoying sales success. What are they doing that you aren't?
3. List the specific things you want to change in order to quit coasting and start pedaling toward advancement.
4. Ask successful people what actions they've taken for their personal self-development.

5.  Create a step-by-step plan to eliminate the coasting gear.
6.  Tell your friends – go public with it – and ask them to hold you accountable.
7.  Have a weekly checkup on your momentum and be honest with yourself.
8.  Celebrate each time you complete one of your self-development programs or goals.

**Results:**
1.  You will now be investing your precious sales time in more productive activity.
2.  As you push for higher standards and increased activity you will start to tap into your sales potential.
3.  You will be shocked and delighted at how much you can do.
4.  You'll uncover more client and prospect needs.
5.  With less downtime and a more focused schedule, your clients and prospects will sense you're in big demand, therefore valuable, and they will want more of you. This is the scarcity factor working for you.

**P.S.** Your commitment to step harder on the pedals and accelerate forward trumps coasting every time.

# COMFORT ZONE

## How to Break Out of Comfort Zones that Keep You a Contented Cow

*"There are risks and costs to a program of action. But they are far less than the long-range risks and costs of comfortable inaction."*
*— John F. Kennedy*

**Premise:**

We all have a variety of comfort zones for different areas of our life. As a sales professional, you must choose to move out of your comfort zone if you want to change and experience real growth. Don't measure yourself against the averages, the prior generations, your neighbor, or how your predecessor performed. He or she might well have been very mediocre! Rather, you must only focus on fully utilizing YOUR personal potential. Until you are pushed, or you push yourself, you will remain in the comfort zone. Go for the end zone and score.

**Symptoms of Impending Disaster:**
- You started out like a house afire with your sales career and then leveled off with no increases in sales.
- You are very comfortable and feel that your income is just fine.
- You never thought you'd make this much money in your life.
- You ask, "Why make the extra sales call when I'm on target to meet my business plan?"
- You find yourself saying, "I'm in the middle group."
- You find yourself thinking, "I've made more money than my Dad ever did."
- You have a big, successful month and then you slack off and fall back into your comfort zone – the real you.

## Story:

As the branch manager of what is now the Smith Barney office in Newport Beach in the 1960's, I was faced with the challenge of motivating Charles, a potential star who was swaddled in his comfort zone. One evening, while discussing his business plan, I asked him what he'd really love to do if he had all the money that he needed. Without hesitation, he said, "Jack, I'd love to have a sailboat and take my family and friends sailing on the weekends."

The next morning, I brought in a picture of a beautiful sailboat and pinned it on the door of his office. Soon, he had written his name on the boat, had put it in a frame and looked at it every day. Yes – he moved out of his old sales comfort zone and into his sailboat. With the wind at his back, he continued to sail into success. But he had to leave the marina first!

## Solutions:

1. Ask yourself: Are you really pushing yourself, or are you just drifting?
2. Are you a bit complacent?
3. Set standards and goals higher than where you are today.
4. Make a commitment to push yourself to higher numbers in activity and in sales.
5. Ask for input from the sales management team.
6. Keep yourself accountable to your commitment to move out of your comfort zone.
7. Make sure that you have strong reasons to move out of your sales comfort zone – family, friends, ego, charity, etc.

## Results:

1. You'll feel that you are fresh and starting to grow again.
2. You will enjoy exceeding your new, higher sales targets.
3. You will start to see more clients and more prospects and find their pain.
4. Your sales and activity numbers will jump off the charts.

5. You will silence those who assumed you had retired on the job.
6. Your paycheck will be fatter.
7. You will gain increased confidence.

**P.S.** Every day, force yourself out of a comfort zone and get uncomfortable. That is where growth takes place.

# RELATIONSHIPS

# TRASHING

## If You Criticize the Competition,
## You Compromise Your Career

*"It's tough to get ahead when you waste your time
getting even." – Lou Holtz*

**Premise:**

In the sales arena, we all want a level playing field that includes information, access, and fairness. It is your responsibility to continue to contribute to the level playing field. Be part of the solution and not part of the problem. Your reputation is a critical part of this opportunity, and a big slice of your reputation lies in refusing to trash the competition. Always take the high road.

**Symptoms of Impending Disaster:**
- During your conversation with clients and prospects, you usually throw out a barb or two about your competition.
- In sales meetings, you lead the cheers to openly bad-mouth the competition.
- When your clients and prospects give you an opening, you jump on the opportunity to make the competition look bad.
- When talking to your competitors, you always knock the ones who are not present.
- When you lose a sale, you typically justify it by finding a fault with your competitor, i.e., they always tell lies regarding their service.
- In social conversation, you gladly join in when some poor soul is being trashed.
- You secretly enjoy trashing people.

**Story:**

I was recently coaching a friend's daughter, who is in the residential real estate business. She had been off to a great start, but was now struggling with excuses. It seemed that when another sales consultant landed a listing or a sale, she always knew how to trash something from their background. Her favorite was a local real estate star who, by chance, had a wealthy mother and father. Of course, to her all of this gentleman's success was because of his heritage. I quickly pointed out this trash talk was a poison to her system, was not well received by her fellow team members, in poor taste and a flat-out excuse.

Upon examination, we both saw that he had created – by himself – the brightness in his star by being a tireless prospector. I told my young student to get out of the trash business and get into the prospecting business. Go out and make calls.

### Solutions:

1. When the thought of trashing the competition enters your mind, have a quick funeral and bury the negative thought.
2. When your client and prospect give you an opening and an opportunity to knock the competition, immediately change the subject of the conversation.
3. Discourage your sale team partners from trashing the competition.
4. Do not participate in group conversation where the competition is being trashed.
5. Bite your tongue if you hear a rumor about a competitor trashing you.
6. Live by the Golden Rule.

### Results:

1. Your clients and prospects will share confidential information with you because they know you won't use it to trash others.
2. Your respect for yourself will go up – especially when you look yourself in the mirror.
3. Your clients and prospects will give you greater trust and respect.
4. Your competition will have an increased respect for you and will be less tempted to ever trash YOU.

5. You will now have the time and energy for positive actions, rather than trying to clean up your act because of trashing someone.

**P.S.** As the IBM district sales manager for the Midwestern states, I laid down a very specific law:  If any of our team members, regardless of their sales success, knocked the competition, I would fire them. More than once I made good on my promise.

# GOSSIP

## How to Overcome the Grip of Gossip:  Small Minds Talking about Small Issues

*"Live in such a way that you would not be ashamed to sell your parrot to the town gossip."*
*— Will Rogers*

**Premise:**

Gossip is a short-term risk that can backfire and destroy client and prospect confidence. When you voluntarily enter the gossip circle, you have chosen to lower your standards and cast your lot with the ordinary. Clients, prospects and team members look for professionals they can share with, learn from, and trust. If you consistently gossip about others in front of a client or prospect, why wouldn't you also gossip about your clients and prospects? You will be consistent, either as a gossiper or as a non-gossiper. It is the nature of man.

**Symptoms of Impending Disaster:**
- You enjoy repeating unkind hearsay about other people.
- You routinely find yourself in groups of people who are primarily focused on disparaging others.
- It makes you feel good when gossip can make others look bad.
- When someone brings up a positive comment regarding another person, you can't resist and give it a, "However, did you know ... ?"
- You remain silent and allow others to attack your friends and associates with malicious gossip without defending them.

**Story:**

During a Christmas Eve party one year, my wife, Judy, overheard another person speaking negatively about a friend of hers. Let me add that two very principled parents schooled Judy on ethics, morality and honest behavior. Judy didn't hesitate to immediately speak up, saying, "Yes, I know who you're talking about. She's my good friend. Please stop maligning her." Instantly, the scuttlebutt about Judy's friend stopped and the person who had started it was clearly embarrassed. The conversation changed, and my partner, Judy, felt good about her simple and timely defense of a friend. That wasn't the last time Judy derailed a gossip train. Stand by your friend, your word and your principles. Don't gossip or allow malicious gossip to move in and take up residence. Don't let your residence be a glass house.

### Solutions:

1.  When tempted to repeat unkind hearsay, stop and ask yourself how you'd feel if you were the topic of gossip.
2.  When hearing rude talk about someone you know, remind yourself of that person's good qualities and you'll find your thoughts instantly becoming more positive in their regard.
3.  Don't participate when others do. Simply change the subject or excuse yourself.
4.  Stick up for your friends, coworkers and partners and tell the truth quickly. You would appreciate the very same being done on your behalf, wouldn't you?
5.  Establish your reputation as a person who chooses not to join the gossip club.
6.  If you're going to say it, be proud to let everyone hear you. Think about that.

### Results:

1.  Your own self-esteem will soar.
2.  What you're doing is good for your soul.
3.  Other people will respect you.
4.  You'll be invited into more open conversations.
5.  You'll be given more trust.
6.  You'll be viewed as a professional.
7.  Your clients and prospects will take note of your professional approach to communication and relationships.

8. Clients and prospects know you will not gossip about them.

**P.S.** Make a choice about the type of mind you will manage: Small minds talk about people, medium minds talk about things and great minds talk about ideas.

# JEALOUSY

## Your Green Envy Smells Rotten – Here's How to Get Rid of the Stench

*"Jealousy is the art of injuring ourselves more than others."*
*– Alexandre Dumas*

**Premise:**

It is natural to want to win at all times, to be at the top in sales and in contests. However, some people just cannot help themselves when it comes to enjoying others' successes. The belief in abundance over scarcity is one of personal choice. One of the defining characteristics between the sales professional and the pretender is the professional's ability to compete successfully without crossing the line into jealousy, when others have a greater measure of success.

**Symptoms of Impending Disaster:**
- You can't congratulate the sales leaders.
- You are resentful and green with envy over other people's successes.
- You are envious of the sales manager's promotions that you believe you deserved.
- When you don't qualify for a sales contest, you announce that it really wasn't important to you.
- When your neighbor buys a great new car, you just dismiss it as a wasteful use of money when, in fact, you wish you had one just like it.
- You always have an alibi when others succeed and you don't.
- You constantly find fault with the leaders in your business.
- You make fun of the sales contests in your firm.
- You have a reputation for being an insecure person.
- You're uncomfortable around other people who are successful.
- When your manager tells you about a successful approach by one of your fellow team members, you quickly add, "Yes, but ..."

**Story:**

As a young boy, we moved often because my Dad was a "fruit tramp," harvesting crops. On Sundays, while Dad was working, Mom would send me to church. While we were in the Phoenix area, and I was attending church, I discovered that they gave gifts to children who had just had a birthday that week. This was May, my birthday was in April and my next birthday was a long 11 months away. But I was envious of these gifts these children received and decided to take action.

The next week, my jealousy got the best of me. When it came time for the birthday announcements, I stood up and announced that I had just had a birthday. Wow! Did my mother give me a talking to and a spanking! Worse, I had to go back to church, return the gift and tell them about my lie.

Jealousy simply does not pay. It removes a measure of one's dignity.

**Solutions:**
1. Examine the source of your jealousy.
2. Congratulate the sales leaders.
3. Take the time to send a handwritten note to others who have succeeded.
4. Bite your tongue when Mr. Jealousy starts to take over your thought process.
5. Mention others' successes in conversations.
6. Re-think your goals as to why you're jealous.
7. Adopt a belief in abundance and not scarcity.

**Results:**
1. You will become a more powerful person.
2. You will be well-liked by the sales management and support teams.
3. No more energy will be wasted on being jealous.
4. You will now learn from others' successes.
5. No more false rivalry.

6. You will be more productive.
7. You will eliminate hostilities from your life.
8. You will be an honest competitor without the negative emotions of jealousy.

**P.S.** Your positive attitude is a painkiller for jealousy.

# DISRESPECTFUL

## How to Cure the Disease of Disrespect

*"I just don't get no respect."* – Rodney Dangerfield

**Premise:**

Respect is the intangible all people seek, especially sales professionals. You can't buy it. In essence, the respect factor is a composite created by all your daily actions and inactions. Disrespect is a disease that will rob you of your opportunities and chase clients and prospects away. A disrespectful individual never gets, nor gives, the respect he or she desperately seeks. To get respect you must be respectful.

**Symptoms of Impending Disaster:**

*   You humiliate the sales support team when they make a mistake.
*   When discussing your sales managers, you never give them any credit.
*   When a client or prospect gives you information in confidence, you immediately tell the world.
*   You ridicule the sales management team for many of the changes they make.
*   You are rude to the rookies and administrative clerks.
*   You have no regard toward rules that concern something as simple as cleaning up in the company lunchroom or coffee room.
*   You constantly interrupt people during conversation.
*   You barge into private meetings in order to voice your opinion.
*   You don't respect client and prospect time, as evidenced when you show up without an appointment or arrive late to meetings.
*   You will usually change the conversation to a subject that suits you, or is about you.
*   You're a "no show" at social events without a courtesy call.

**Story:**

My first real leadership opportunity in the business world occurred in the summer of 1954 when I managed a melon-picking crew one summer in Parker, Arizona. The crews were made up of tough, hungry, hard-working Mexicans in this country on a work program. My father, who had started as a field worker, understood real work and had instilled in me the importance of treating the field workers with respect.

On Saturdays, I would help them get money orders to send cash home to their families because many couldn't write. Days were long and hot and we started at sun-up. I made it clear to my crew leaders that they were to take care of the men and treat them with respect. It soon became apparent, however, that Tommy, one of the crew leaders, was taking delight in humiliating his crew members if they accidentally dropped a melon, and he joked about their lack of education.

Remembering my Dad's words of wisdom, I confronted Tommy one day and fired him on the spot. For a brief moment, I thought a fight was going to erupt between the two of us. At that moment, the crew stood up as one and smiled in my direction. Tommy knew that respect had won the day. There is no place for disrespect, except last place.

**Solutions:**
1. Sincerely admire the accomplishments of your sales support team.
2. Honor the success of other sales team members.
3. Never repeat something given to you in confidence.
4. Always keep appointments with your clients and prospects.
5. Arrive early for meetings.
6. Seek ways to respect all people.
7. Use the Golden Rule.
8. Bite your tongue when you start interrupting.
9. Always support your sales management team.

**Results:**
1.  You will immediately get better cooperation.
2.  You will have a reputation as being a respectful and respected individual.
3.  Clients and prospects will respect your professionalism in making appointments and keeping them.
4.  Your sales management team will give you respect.
5.  You will respect yourself.

**P.S.** The Respect Factor™ is the secret sauce for sales professionals.

# GREEDY

## Don't Let Greed Kill the Goose That Laid the Golden Egg

*"Thinking to get at once all the gold that the goose could give, he killed it and opened it ...only to find nothing." — Aesop*

**Premise:**

No one chooses to spend his or her time with greedy people. To seek success is natural, but to have a need to hoard riches and material things is a disease. In the movie "Wall Street," actor Michael Douglas, during a speech to stockholders, said, "Greed is good ... it works." In the end, greed destroyed him. In real life, Ivan Boesky of Wall Street fame also commented that greed was healthy. Shortly thereafter, he paid the price for his greed and went to prison. A critical part of the success opportunity is sharing with others.

**Symptoms of Impending Disaster:**
- Your charity contributions total one word – cheap.
- The local waitresses avoid you because you're known as the "No-Tipper."
- Your sales management asks you to divide up accounts from a recently parted sales team member. You get greedy and take the most and the best.
- When there's a split in the bill for a meal, you don't give your share.
- You always think of yourself first.
- You have no time to share your experiences with the rookies.
- You will not invest your money in yourself for self-development.
- You wouldn't consider taking the administrative staff out to lunch.

**Story:**

In Sun Valley, Idaho, I had the opportunity to attend the

memorial service for one of the local giants who had contributed significantly to our quality of life, Bill Janss. He had built his reputation on being a giver and helping his fellow man. At his service, Guy Bonivier, the manager for the Idaho Nature Conservancy, shared a special story.

At a prior time, Bill had given a very valuable section of the Silver Creek area to the Nature Conservancy. It was a highly desirable piece of land – beautiful, quiet and teeming with giant rainbow trout. At the same time, Bill wrote a large, six-figure check and contributed to the conservancy.

When Bill wrote the check, Guy said, "Bill, you don't have to give money in addition to the land!" Bill responded, "Well, Guy, when you open the refrigerator and have three quarts of milk on the shelf and you can only drink one, you should share your good fortune with others."

## Solutions:
1. Establish a percentage of your income to be given to charity.
2. Get involved with a charity.
3. Invest your money and time in others.
4. Examine your values and goals as they relate to charity.
5. Consider the needs of others when you're hoarding supplies.
6. Encourage others to get involved in sharing their time and resources.
7. Ask your clients and prospects what charitable organizations they're involved in that might need help from you.
8. Reach out and help someone in your firm with an educational opportunity.
9. Be a leader in your company to rein in greed.

## Results:
1. You will help others by sharing your time and wealth.
2. You will experience increased respect from your friends, sales support team, sales management team, clients and prospects.
3. Clients and prospects will ask you to help their charitable

interests.

4.  You will feel better about yourself. It is truly better to give than receive.
5.  You will meet interesting and worthwhile people.
6.  You'll be exposed to new opportunities.

**P.S.** "Earn all you can, save all you can, give all you can." – John Wesley

# SELFISH

## You Are Your Brother's Keeper

*"For what is a man profited if he shall gain the whole world
and lose his own soul?" – Matthew 16:26*

**Premise:**

We all need help in our personal and professional lives. Remember, you will not always have all the right solutions at the right time, in the right place. You have a choice to extend a helping hand to your friends, team members and clients or, instead, pull back to navigate the road to success completely alone – and that's a long, lonely road.

**Symptoms of Impending Disaster:**

- You never volunteer to help others.
- You feel that you are too busy to take your valuable time to help others.
- You never ask to be given the tough job assignments.
- You resent it when you are asked to do something that you see as "extra" and not part of your job description.
- You consistently have a view of "Me vs. Them" as you approach tasks.
- You're extremely self-centered.
- You never work for a charity.
- When there's a short supply of materials, you always take more than your share.
- Your reputation is that you have good numbers, but you're selfish.

**Story:**

I have always viewed my sales team members as family. While making calls one day in Salt Lake City with one of our new sales team members, Todd, I asked a family-type question and received a wake-up-call answer. I asked, "Todd, how's your family?" He turned away, bowed his head and said that his father was seriously ill with cancer. His chances for survival were slim.

From that moment, I made an effort to spend more time with Todd. I also made sure that I had the opportunity to meet his mother and father and tell them what a fine young man they had raised.

When that final day arrived and Todd's father passed away, four of my sales team members called and offered to help Todd in any way, including making sales calls and working in Todd's territory without any compensation while Todd helped his family during his demanding time. It wasn't their job, but they were there for a peer and a friend.

### Solutions:

1. Every day, look for action you can take to help other people.
2. Ask your sales manager if he or she has any responsibilities that can be offloaded to you.
3. Volunteer to mentor one of the new sales team members.
4. Offer to role-play with other sales team members.
5. Get involved in a charity.
6. Ask the sales manager if you can help with upcoming sales meetings.
7. Go to the sales support team and ask how you can help them.
8. Always apply the Golden Rule: Do unto others as you would have them do unto you.

### Results:

1. You will gain increased respect from your peers.
2. You will make a real difference in people's lives.
3. You will receive unexpected help from your team members.
4. You will like the person in the mirror and you will feel good about yourself.

**P.S**. Every day, we all have to help each other up the ladder of life.

# TEAM

## You Win When Your Team Wins

*"For the strength of the pack is the wolf. And the strength of the wolf is the pack." — Rudyard Kipling*

**Premise:**

Every day, people help me on my journey. Certainly the world is a better place because people help each other. Can you imagine how you could have progressed through life if people had not given you a helping hand from time to time?

While I'm sure you nod your head in agreement, I very often observe the exact opposite in action in a sales-oriented environment. From basic disinterest to stubborn refusal to participate in the group or help other team members in any way, this lone wolf attitude tears at the fundamental elements of sales success. The lone wolf attitude is a short-term solution. The team player should, instead, rely on the power of the team to help him or her move up the sales mountain.

**Symptoms of Impending Disaster:**
- Rookies ask you for direction and you don't have the time.
- Your sales manager calls you to conduct the sales meeting and you agree, but give it very little attention or planning effort, and the results prove it.
- A team member was given a retirement party but you opted out for a round of golf instead.
- At team sales meetings, you offer zero input.
- The word "team" is not in your vocabulary.
- The company's bottom line results are not important to you.
- Clients and prospects know you won't seek input and solutions from your company.
- You don't seem to have any real friends in the company.
- You choose not to share new and exciting solutions you have discovered with your team members.

- When you're asked to role-play with one of your team members, you say you're too busy.
- You have a reputation for being a self-centered individual.

**Story:**

At Manulife Wood Logan, I've had the good fortune to associate with some of the very best wholesalers in the world, as evidenced by client surveys. One such rising star in my division was Steve Scanlon. We often invested Sunday afternoons in phone meetings concerning sales strategy. These phone conversations were just part of his committed work ethic. He was a true workhorse; he was a sales leader, an income leader, and always busy with big-time demands from his customers and prospects. However, he always gave the big "Yes" when asked to help train new team members and share his keys to success. He was always available to talk to those in need, even the rookies. He traveled out of his territory to give company presentations because he was one of the best presenters, and it seemed the more time he gave the team, the more he received personally. You could say his real name was Steve "Team" Scanlon, a true partner.

**Solutions:**

1. Ask your sales manager how you can help the team.
2. Ask the rookies if they need assistance.
3. Volunteer to help others in role playing.
4. Every day, look for at least one new opportunity to help.
5. Think of "success" as providing more for everyone, because that's exactly where success starts.
6. Think "We" and not just "Me."
7. Get to know your sales team members.
8. Actively participate in the sales meetings.
9. Encourage your sales team members.
10. Share your successful ideas.
11. Share your plans with your sales support team.
12. Give credit and praise to other team members.

13. Ask your sales support team members to share their goals with you.
14. Write thank-you notes.

**Results:**
1. You will feel better about yourself by helping others.
2. You will help improve overall sales, both for the team and for yourself.
3. Your team members will respect and seek you out.
4. You will acquire new levels of confidence and success.
5. You will learn and profit from your team members.
6. Clients and prospects will expect you to go the highest level in your company to help solve their problems.
7. You will change people's lives.
8. You will enjoy the reputation of being a team player.
9. With your new "We" attitude, you will experience greater cooperation, which leads to greater success.

**P.S.** It's time to focus on abundance for all. Ask yourself, "What can I share with my team members that will help them along their journey to success?"

# RUDE

## Your Reputation for Rudeness Can Result in Your Being Fired!

*"Civility costs nothing." — Anonymous*

**Premise:**

There is absolutely no room in a successful business for rude behavior. It's all right to disagree with a client, prospect or sales team member, but it is not acceptable when rudeness on your part accompanies that disagreement. Discourteous behavior will cost you friendships, business and opportunities.

**Symptoms of Impending Disaster:**

- You are frequently ill-mannered.
- You have a reputation for being discourteous.
- You think polite people are just afraid to speak up.
- You are known for interrupting social conversations.
- In your sales meetings, you choose to talk to your buddies while the sales manager is trying to make a point that would help you increase your business.
- You arrive unannounced to meet with clients and prospects.
- You walk into the sales manager's office while he's on the phone.

**Story:**

As an orphan, my Mom had to fight for all her opportunities and taught my sister and me a proper competitive attitude. In that teaching, she always insisted that we be polite, regardless of the situation.

One blistering summer day, we were at the Greyhound Bus station in Blythe, California, waiting in line for the next bus. We were hot, the queue was long, and people were edgy. They announced that they had oversold the bus and that some people were going to have to wait even longer for a much later arrival. Suddenly, a real jerk came up from the back of the line, and elbowed his way in front of my mother, a true lady. When people behind us told him he wasn't acting fairly, he responded loudly with inappropriate language. Much to my surprise, Mom immediately grabbed him and hit him right in the face. He was so shocked that he stumbled back, lost his footing, and was grabbed and held by our fellow passengers until the police arrived to escort him away. Mr. Rude got a free ride to the police station; I proudly sat next to my Mom on the bus.

## Solutions:
1. Make a list of all the ways you can be rude and the ways you can be polite, then bury the rude actions and embrace the opportunity to be polite.
2. Always make appointments with your clients and prospects.
3. If you have an urgent need, ask if you can interrupt your sales manager for a moment; otherwise, take your turn.
4. Don't interrupt when someone is speaking to you.
5. Find a way to compliment others on their polite behavior.
6. If you ever are rude, examine why and immediately apologize.
7. Seek out ways to be polite, to go the extra distance.

## Results:
1. Clients and prospects will take note of your courteous behavior.
2. You will become more likeable – a key success in sales.
3. Your sales team members will respond to you with courteous behavior.
4. You will experience less personal stress.
5. Because you no longer interrupt people, you will be a more effective communicator.

**P.S.** If you are rude, you will have to ask for pardons.

# POLITICS

## How to Put Politics in its Proper Place

*"In order to become the master, the politician poses as the servant."*
*— Charles DeGaulle*

**Premise:**

Practically speaking, politics has a place in life; it is certainly part of our local, state, and federal governments. We often hear of elected officials who make compromises with fellow peers or elected officials to get legislation passed, such as, "I will vote for your bridge if you vote for my highway," but that sort of compromise should stay in that political arena, not in your own office. The SALES politician is not trading bridges for highways, but rather his respect for a personal favor with the boss. There is absolutely no need to compete with your fellow sales people for favors from management.  Beware of the glad-hander.

**Symptoms of Impending Disaster:**
- You always rush to sit by the big brass at the luncheon meeting.
- You always agree and agree and agree with the boss even though you might not really agree.
- If the boss doesn't like it, you don't like it.
- You are jealous when other sales team members catch the big boss' eye.
- You purposely withhold vital information from the team so you can tell the big boss personally.
- Your motives are usually selfish.
- Your associates talk behind your back regarding your obvious political needs.

**Story:**

In 1965, I was part of a team making a computer presentation to a governmental unit in downtown Chicago for a major computer system. It was decision time. The project was ready to close, the presentation had gone well, and the city officials had nothing but praise for our specific solutions.

As we were preparing to leave the meeting, I asked the city manager what the next step would be at this time. He responded, "Jack, you have given us an excellent solution. But if Mayor Daley doesn't like your proposal, then we don't like it either." Spoken like a true politician.

## Solutions:
1. Observe "politicians" in action and learn what not to do.
2. Ask your manager for the truth regarding your tendency to act like a politician.
3. Ask the same of your friends.
4. Make it a point to have the real you respond when asked a question.
5. Speak up to the boss, regardless of what you think the impact might be.
6. Check your motives regarding your communication with your boss or teammates.
7. Remember: No secret agendas.

## Results:
1. You will start to like yourself better because you're being the real you – no more split personality, always currying favor.
2. You will not be wasting your energy and resources on false positions.
3. You will experience increased trust from your teammates and management.
4. You will contribute to better company decisions.
5. Your boss and associates will benefit from your candor.
6. Your clients and prospects respect the fact that you do the right thing, regardless of the consequences.
7. No one has to wonder about your agenda.

**P.S.** If you want to be a politician, run for an office. If you choose to be a sales professional, aspire to have greater sales activity.

# EGO

## Your Ego is Enormous and Out of Control

*"Gentlemen, I want you to know that I'm not always right,*
*but I am never wrong." — Samuel Goldwyn*

### Premise:

Having strong self-esteem is an essential component of the successful salesperson's mind-set. Without it, you will allow the rejection disease to enter your mind and take up permanent residence, which eventually leads you down the path of failure. But, remember this: Those with the best self-esteem have great skill at keeping it to themselves! If you're not careful, your publicly-demonstrated ego will destroy your potential success.

### Symptoms of Impending Disaster:

- The "I" word is your favorite and most used word.
- You always have the need to trump the other person's story.
- Your conversations are a long one-way street.
- You're beginning to discover that people aren't interested in conversing with you. You bore them.
- At social functions, if you weren't center stage, you didn't have a good time.
- Within five minutes of meeting you, a person has heard about your personal and professional success directly from you.

### Story:

In the early 1960s in the Los Angeles office for IBM, we had a charming account representative there with an ego twice the size of his performance. We used to tell each other that if we could buy George for what he was actually worth and then sell George for what he thought he was worth, we'd all make a quick fortune and retire early. After the influence and charm wore off, and his big "I" took center stage, the sub-performance sales numbers made a glaring statement. Eventually, he was asked to take his "I" act down the street.

## Solutions:

1. Have great self-esteem and keep it to yourself.
2. Let your results do the talking.
3. Every time you start to say "I," ask yourself:
   a. "Is there a better way to say this?
   b. Is this necessary?
   c. Does this help or hurt me?"
4. Put your "I" in the closet and take out your good, long-term close friends, "WE" and "YOU."
5. Use questions to get others to do the talking.
6. When someone shares a success story with you, ask them to expand on it, "Tell me more ... now tell me some more."
7. When asked about your success, quickly answer and get the focus back to the person in front of you with a question about him or her.
8. Get clients and prospects to talk about themselves, their company and their needs.

## Results:

1. Your peers will share more of their ideas and their confidences with you because they see you are involved with more than your life alone.
2. Your clients and prospects will feel you're on the same playing field and will share more important information with you.
3. As a result of being less needy for attention and pats on the back, you will focus more of your energy on finding solutions for your clients and prospects.
4. Your clients, prospects and peers will tell others how they enjoy associating with you.
5. With your ego safely stowed away, you will learn important information about your clients and prospects to help you in the sales process.

**P.S.** Give your ego a rest and learn to cater to others. Listen to others.

# ACTION PLANS

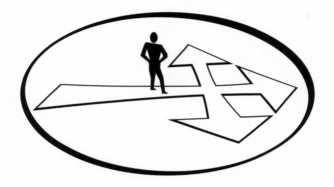

# PRIORITIES
## Don't Major in the Minors!

*"Set priorities for your goals. A major part of successful living lies in the ability to put first things first. Indeed, the reason most major goals are not achieved is that we spend our time doing second things first."*
— Robert J. McKain

**Premise:**
Every day you get up and react to the events of the day – social phone call interruptions from family and friends, "C" and "D" type prospects chewing up your valuable time, and random events creating your schedule. As a result your day gets filled with garbage.

By choosing your priorities, you are clearing a path for your objectives and building a brick wall to defend against interruptions, those hated occurrences that steal your precious time.

**Symptoms of Impending Disaster:**
- You do not have a written "To Do" list.
- You have not established priorities for your day's activity.
- All tasks seem to have the same importance in your mind.
- Every morning, you are lingering over your newspaper in order to avoid getting on with the business of selling. Selling should be the number one priority of the day.
- You avoid the most important tasks of the day and, as a result, they keep reappearing day after day.
- You never tackle the most pressing task and do it first.
- Your 10-minute coffee break has become a pilgrimage to Starbucks.
- You routinely hand deliver non-urgent brochures to "C" and "D" type prospects.
- You find yourself consistently late for client and prospect meetings because of your personal activities.
- Your recent issue of *Sports Illustrated* has been memorized

cover-to-cover while your invaluable *Selling Power* magazine is still in its wrapper.

**Story:**

When I was a college freshman at UCLA, my roommate for the first semester was Brett. He was brilliant and he had earned all A's in his pre-college days. He had participated in athletics, and had also been active in student government. It seemed he had his priorities in place.

Oddly, though, the characteristics that seemed to have earned him such high rankings in high school had disappeared in college. Brett always seemed to be shining his shoes, considering what he would take next year, getting ready to study, going out for pizza and shooting the bull with his fraternity brothers. At the end of his freshman year with grades at the "D" and "F" level, he was asked not to return. He did second things first. He had paid a high price in failing to establish his priorities.

**Solutions:**
1. Before you start your day, prepare a list of your chosen activities, calls, appointments, and "To Do's."
2. Prioritize your events of the day by A, B or C, and then rank each of them in numerical sequence under each primary category with 1, 2, 3, and so forth, i.e., A-1, A-2, B-1, B-2, etc. Now, you know exactly where to start.
3. Start at the top and work down in sequence and avoid the temptation to jump to the bottom of your list because it's easier.
4. Enjoy checking tasks off of your priority list as you complete them.

**Results:**
1. You will have fewer raging forest fires in your mind.
2. You'll have a sharper focus.
3. You will accomplish the important things first.

4. During your day, you will experience less procrastination.
5. You will use your precious time more effectively.
6. At your day's end, you will experience satisfaction of knowing you have used your energy and resources on the right priorities.
7. You will accomplish more.

**P.S.** Have the discipline to keep your chosen priorities in line.

# ORGANIZATION

## Is Disorganization Decimating Your Success?
## How to Conquer Clutter

*"Science is organized knowledge. Wisdom is organized life."*
*— Immanuel Kant*

**Premise:**

Being organized is a personal choice and a process. As a result, you can choose to abandon any discipline associated with organization, such as throwing your clothes and documents into separate piles. You can also allow the events of the day to take over your day. However, if you value your time as the precious commodity it is, you will embrace organization and the many benefits associated with valuing your time. The price you pay to be organized will pay you dividends through increased efficiency. Improve organization, improve your chances for success.

How would you feel if you walked into a doctor's office and saw his desk piled high with clutter? Scary thought.

**Symptoms of Impending Disaster:**
- Your car is usually dirty and messy.
- You're suffering from BJ: Briefcase Jam. Each night when you leave your office, and each morning when you head out of your house, you're just stuffing all the files and papers you've been setting aside into that briefcase. It's simply become a remote "In Box" for you.
- Your reports are usually late and disorganized.
- People complain that you're slow at returning phone calls.
- Your desk looks like the city recycling center. You have a similar pile on your desk at home.

**Story:**

When I worked for IBM in the early 1960s, I first learned about the company's many and specific rules of conduct and appearance.

Remember, IBM represented the concept of accessing information quickly, accurately and successfully; the organization expected its members to walk the talk. The rule as it related to your desk was this: "The desk must be clean when you are not present." In those days, if your desk was left with a mess on it, our branch manager would have the cleaning crew dump the contents into the trash can. To this day, I still conform to the IBM Clean Desk Rule. It's not always easy to accomplish, but it ensures a fresh start when I return.

**Solutions:**
1. There are many organizational systems available today such as the Franklin Day Planner, Daytimer or Palm Pilot. Like any system, you have to invest in it, and then devote time to learning how to use it. Then: Use it.
2. You want to own and be able to operate your CRM – Client Relationship Management system – forward and backward.
3. When you go after the day's opportunities each business morning, the following should be accomplished the previous evening before you go to bed:
   a. Your clothes are laid out.
   b. Your car is clean.
   c. No more Briefcase Jam; in fact, it should look as if it's on a diet.
   d. Your days and weeks are planned in terms of specific geographic locations.
   e. You know where you're going that day and that week, with whom you're meeting, and what are your target goals.
   f. You know your story.
4. At the end of each day, you're organized for tomorrow.
5. On Sunday evening, you have your game face on and are organized for the week ahead.

**Results:**
1. You'll experience significantly less stress.
2. You will save enormous amounts of time.

3.  You have more energy available for the sales process.
4.  You'll find you're more productive.
5.  You will be able to see more prospects.
6.  Responsibilities come your way because you've proven you have the time allotted to take them on.

**P.S.** In its simplest form, being organized brings you more options.

# TIME

## Turbo-Charge Your Time to Avoid Being Terminated

*"Until you value yourself, you will not value your time. Until you value your time, you will not do anything about it."*
*— Dr. M. Scott Peck*

**Premise:**

Don't tell me you don't have the time to practice, read and see more clients and prospects. We all have been allocated the same 24 hours, seven days a week. You cannot hoard or save it. You cannot control or manage time, but you can manage events. We have the time; it's a matter of where we choose to invest it. Therefore, consider how you invest blocks of time: how much time for breakfast and lunch, how much time for administration, how much time for selling. Take pride in investing your time in your career and your company.

**Symptoms of Impending Disaster:**
*   You don't plan your time investments.
*   You're always saying, "Sometime, when I get the time ... "
*   You frequently decline opportunities with the response, "I don't have enough time."
*   Your scratch pad or Daytimer is jammed with personal items.
*   You do too many things you could delegate to someone else.
*   You're having frequent, long conversations with friends during business hours.
*   You frequently say, "I don't know where my time goes."
*   You linger over those coffee breaks.
*   You frequently have to leave new projects because you didn't allocate the best time to do it correctly the first time around.
*   You are not controlling the events in your life.
*   You let people drop into your office just to chat.
*   You keep poor records of how you actually invest your time.

**Story:**

Stan, a young friend of mine in the financial services industry, often came to me for mentoring and advice for the future. I could see that with Stan's work ethic and moral fiber, he had a wide road ahead in the sales profession.

One day over a quick lunch, I asked Stan what he was doing about getting his Series 24 qualification. He leaned back in the booth, holding out his hands in dismay. "Jack," he said, "I just don't have time right now. You know these things are hard; they take a lot of study time. My mom's really ill and she needs my time and attention. Shoot! I want to get my CFP, too, but this just isn't the time." Feeling sympathetic, I let it go. My mistake.

Months later in October, Stan and I were at a conference together and grabbed a cup of coffee during a break. "How's your mom doing?" I asked. "Much better," was the reply. I guess my raised brow gave me away; Stan anticipated my question about the Series 24 and the CFP. "I know, Jack, I know." He shrugged, grinned and told me that he and his wife were expecting another child in the spring and that his plate would be really full at home. "My time's pretty much spoken for this next year." I reminded him that Dr. Donald Moine, author of *Unlimited Selling Power*, has often said that Americans love credentials. They count.

I saw a crestfallen Stan the following summer at a golf tournament. At the turn, I asked what was bothering him. "I was passed over for a Regional Manager position on the West Coast," he groaned. Sheepishly, he asked, "Know why? They wanted someone with a CFP." Hands raised, he said, "Don't say it. I'm kicking myself hard enough!"

If only Stan had had the time. If only.

**Solutions:**
1. Learn to value your time.
2. Invest in the necessary tools – a Palm Pilot, Daytimer or Franklin Planner, a client relations management system, and an appropriate filing system.

3.  Be aware of how you are using your time.
4.  For just one week, keep a record of the number of hours you are actively engaged in your profession. No cheating! These hours or quarter-hours can't include phone calls home, e-mails to friends, or various other schedules and appointments in your personal life.
5.  For the next 30 days, at the end of each day, record the time you are actually in front of prospects and customers, selling to them.
6.  Keep social calls and e-mails to a minimum.
7.  Keep those time robbers away from the golden selling hours of 8 to 5.
8.  Have a Do Not Disturb sign for your office. Use it.
9.  Lock out times for your various types of activities.
10. Remember to always think "First Things First."
11. Don't procrastinate.
12. Get organized and stay organized.

**Results:**
1.  You will be able to use your time more productively.
2.  You will now know how much time you're investing in business, and how much time you're investing in "other" activities.
3.  Your sales activity will increase.
4.  You will feel better about how you are using your most valuable commodity – your time.
5.  Your time will be invested by choice and not default.
6.  You'll have more free time to invest as you choose.

**P.S.** You cannot manage time, but you can control the events in your life.

# ENERGY

## Your Energy Has Lost Its Power and Force

*"Energy is the essence of life. Every day you decide how you're going to use it by knowing what you want and what it takes to reach that goal, and by maintaining focus." — Oprah Winfrey*

**Premise:**

You're issued only one body in your lifetime. The way you treat your body is on a parallel with how your body will treat you. Poor nutritional intake, coupled with your primary exercise being typing e-mail to your friends, is a fast track to the Couch Potato Hall of Fame. Would you bet on a racehorse that had a steady diet of junk food, lay on the soft straw in her stall all day, and watched horse opera on the TV while her competitors were working out aggressively on the track? No way.

You must put the energy into your body, just as you put high octane fuel in the tank of a high-performance Jaguar.

**Symptoms of Impending Disaster:**
- You're turning off your alarm every morning and sleeping in.
- You're tired at 10 a.m. and tired at 3 p.m.
- You typically fall asleep in meetings.
- You never volunteer for challenging tasks because they seem overwhelming.
- You maintain that everything's difficult. Life is so stressful.
- At the end of the day, you're too tired to make that extra call.
- You enjoy watching mindless midnight TV.
- You prefer junk foods and sweets to protein and vegetables.
- Your workout clothes are somewhere deep in the storage unit. At least they're in good shape – from lack of use.

**Story:**

During a client educational program in Sedona, Arizona, one morning I chose to get an early workout before the meeting. I made my way to the fitness center, down a dark path before sunrise. As I opened the door with my key, to my surprise I noticed one of my younger competitors was already there and had worked up a sweat on the treadmill.

Not to be intimidated, I jumped on the rowing machine and turned it up. Of course, out of the corner of my eye, I couldn't help but notice that my morning workout companion began running at a faster rate. After 30 minutes at a full sweat, I realized that he was going to outwork me this morning. While I pride myself with an abundance of energy, I had met my match. Quietly, I got off the rowing machine and slipped out the back door. He was still running.

In the following days, I got to know Darren and his wife, Jo. It soon became evident that his energy came from his disciplined lifestyle and commitment. Even today when I see Darren, I say to myself, "Mr. Energy." It paid off. I had the opportunity to recruit him to our team and he now manages a most successful sales division for our firm.

**Solutions:**

1.  Eat properly in terms of food choices and quantity, plus consider seeking out a nutritionist for advice. A large part of your energy is based on what you eat. In the book, *The Power of Full Engagement* by Jim Loehr and Tony Schwartz, scores of athletes were tested and found to have the following habits in common. They were:

   a.  Eat whole grains, proteins and fresh fruits.
   b.  Skip bagels and juice filled with sugar.
   c.  Maintain portion control.
   d.  Drink full glasses of water at least eight times a day. By the time you're thirsty you're already dehydrated.
   e.  Skip coffee.
   f.  Go to bed early and wake up early.
   g.  Institute and stick to a regular exercise program.
   h.  Take a break every 90 minutes, call a loved one, take a walk, and even jump up and down.

2. Breathe deeply and abdominally.
3. Commit to a daily exercise program.
4. Join a fitness center or establish a fitness center in your own home.
5. Consider a personal trainer. They force fitness upon you!
6. Consider taking vitamins every day.
7. Have periodic physical examinations.

**Results:**
1. You'll have increased energy in all phases of your life.
2. You'll add energy to all your business and personal relationships.
3. You'll have the energy to stretch yourself, seek more opportunities and have more fun, and enjoy more experiences in life.
4. You will make more calls and see more clients and prospects.
5. When you walk in the room, the energy level of the room goes up. It's catching.
6. People comment on your energy and ask, "Where does it come from?"
7. You will have the energy to help others.

**P.S.** Turn your energy switch on "High."

# ACTIVITY

## Your Activity Report Needs to Take Action!

*"As I grow older, I pay less attention to what men say.
I just watch what they do." — Andrew Carnegie*

**Premise:**

Sales is an action sport.

There's no question that if you're in the sales game, a significant measure of your sales success will be related to your daily rock-and-roll activity, the number of contacts, the number of meetings, the number of presentations. What are you really doing out there today? If you don't keep accurate records on your activity, how do you know what you are worth? How do you know what is and is not working for you? It isn't enough to go home tired and say, "I've worked hard." Remember the Law of Reciprocity, which says that for every action there is an equal and opposite reaction. All professional sales success starts with the numbers game. No big numbers, no big sales. That simple.

**Symptoms of Impending Disaster:**

- At the end of the day, week or month, your number of sales contacts is low.
- More importantly, your sales calls are falling below your personal target and your company's target.
- You've noticed that you're starting your days later and quitting earlier each afternoon.
- Late in the day, when it's time to make the additional call, you find yourself inwardly saying that your activity is already good enough.
- You don't experience any anxiety when clients or prospects cancel an appointment and your contact numbers are down.
- Your activity records are not up-to-date, they are inaccurate, and in your mind sales activity records are just an exercise for sales management.

- You're not concerned that your activity ranks at the bottom of your company and your team.

## Story:

As a new financial advisor in the mid-1960s, I was very serious and committed to record keeping for my target numbers vs. actual calls. Back then, we didn't have the luxury of an Excel spreadsheet or contact management software, so I created an activity book wherein I kept track of my daily, weekly and monthly totals. As an example, I knew how many prospects or clients by category I talked to on the phone, how many I met face-to-face, and the number of business lunches and dinners I hosted. I also tracked how many seminars I conducted, the number of attendees, the number of appointments and the results.

At the end of each day, if I had not exceeded my activity targets by category, I was disgusted with my performance. With this system staring me in the face every day, I progressively topped my targets and experienced greater, faster success.

## Solutions:

1. Accept the fact that all successful selling is a Numbers Game.
2. Create a weekly and monthly sales call target that requires you to have a full schedule at the start of each week prior to Monday morning. It's the only way you're going to grow.
3. Get your appointment schedule full of quality appointments, not quantity, and keep it there at all times.
4. Maintain current and accurate daily, weekly and monthly activity records vs. your company and personal target numbers.
5. Commit to never quitting until you've reached and surpassed your call activity targets. Never, never quit.

## Results:

1. You will be wisely investing your most valuable commodity – time – and you'll be using it more effectively.
2. You'll help more people solve their challenges and, in so doing,

will feel better personally about yourself.

3.  It's basic math: the odds are with you. You're going to have more opportunity for a home run if you go to bat more often.

4.  You'll experience greater sales success and greater satisfaction.

5.  Your income will rapidly move north.

6.  You will keep your sales manager aligned with you and your competitors at bay.

**P.S.** Remember, the age-old formula still works: **P x E = S.**

P = Number of presentations you choose to make

E = Effectiveness of your presentations

S = Sales

# DECISIONS

## How to Slay Decision Dragons

*"Life is an endless change of judgments ... the more imperfect our judgment, the less perfect our success."*
*— B. C. Forbes*

**Premise:**

Every day in the sales world we're faced with a continuous stream of decisions. Where do you invest your time and resources? Whom do you call on? How do you solve the requests for your resources? While it may seem that you've got to act on the fly just to keep the wheels turning, it's far better in the long run to approach your decision making with a process. Using a consistent process for your sales decisions will give you the opportunity to make better decisions and get better results.

**Symptoms of Impending Disaster:**
- You usually make hasty decisions.
- In disputes, you always decide in favor of the client or prospect vs. the company.
- Many of your decisions are routinely reversed by the management team.
- Your decision path is locked onto the course of least resistance.
- You rarely ask others for input on major client and prospect decisions.

**Story:**

As the CEO for United Resources, I had a manager in Cleveland who was too quick when it came to making decisions. He acted immediately, never thought things through and, in fact, took pride in being known for his decision making speed. Finally, after meeting with his sales team for a quarterly review of the office, it became apparent that a potential revolt was developing because this manager made rash decisions without fully considering the impact they would have on the sales team.

I had the manager begin to use a very simple form for all of his key decisions. It included points such as:

- Do I know the impact this will have on all team members?
- Is this fair and is it in the best interest of the client or prospect and our mutual profitability?
- With whom should I consult?

**Solutions:**

1. Have you gathered ALL the pertinent facts that impact your decisions?
2. As appropriate, ask for advice and input – then listen.
3. Ask yourself, "Is this a decision for me? Should it be made by the sales management team or the sales support team?"
4. Write your decision choices on paper. In so doing, you're giving your mind clarity to evaluate each possible solution and its effects separately.
5. If time permits on major decisions, consider sleeping on it and acting the next day.
6. Make a decision.
7. Explain your decision to those individuals involved and allow them to comment.
8. Act and go forward. Don't second-guess yourself.
9. If it turns out that you should make a modification or reverse a previous decision, be strong enough to act and do it. Everyone concerned will benefit.

**Results:**

1. You will learn from your good decisions and your poor decisions. Everyone does.
2. You will be a more confident and decisive decision maker.
3. You will be faced with very few reversals of your decisions.
4. People will not hesitate to come to you for help in making sound decisions.

5. Because your business is based on sound decisions, your sales will increase.

**P.S.** The only hard decisions are the ones you don't think through.

## PROSPECTING

### How to Distinguish Fool's Gold from Real Gold
### When You Prospect

*"In the sales profession, you either constantly prospect with a plan or you subconsciously implement your early retirement plan."*
*— Jack Perry*

**Premise:**

The lifeblood of all successful business is clients, and more of them. From CPA's to heart surgeons to real estate brokers to financial planners to investment technicians – you will always need to convert prospects to clients. Why? Because no matter how good you are, you will lose some of your existing clients along the way. People's lives change, and in order to maintain and grow your business, you need to be adding qualified prospects and clients constantly.

**Symptoms of Impending Disaster:**

- You are shuffling the same old prospect cards day after day.
- While you list prospecting for new clients as a priority, you seem to find a way to put it off for tomorrow.
- When asked how you prospect, you respond, "Oh, I only expand my business through satisfied referrals."
- You can't stand the rejection you feel from a client or prospect who tells you "No," so you stop altogether.
- You choose not to believe that sales is a numbers game. The very thought offends you; you are a professional.
- You quickly drop qualified prospects when they give you the big "No."

**Story:**

In 1968 while managing the Los Angeles branch for a major financial services firm, I had a young, future superstar named Michael on my team. Mike accepted a leadership position as manager of our Santa Barbara office.

When Mike arrived for his first sales meeting in Santa Barbara, he sat down at the conference table and gave all the financial planners in the room a picture of a coffin at a funeral. He looked them in the eye and said, "Suppose this is your biggest client: What are you going to do?" I am sure most of the brokers were stunned and some were offended, but the point is this: Mike was doing the right thing. Clients will retire and, eventually, clients will also pass away. If you don't have a solid prospecting funnel in place, your income could be dramatically shifted downward with the loss of just one or two major clients. Ironically, 10 years later in that same office, a friend of mine, Richard, had the opportunity to respond to that exact experience: His biggest client died and he wasn't prepared. Richard had to scramble. Mike went on to become the managing director for the largest division of one of the most powerful financial services firms in the world.

## Solutions:
1. Accept prospecting as the gospel for sales success.
2. Love to prospect.
3. Select your prospecting system and stick with it.
4. Prospect regularly.
5. Establish specific prospecting goals.
6. Put your goals in front of your eyes every day.
7. Each week, maintain accurate prospecting records.
8. Each week and month, keep on prospecting after you achieve your prospecting goals.
9. Keep honest and accurate prospecting records.
10. Practice your prospecting skills. Stay sharp, just as a golfer does with his game.
11. Don't quit prospecting until you exceed your goals.

## Results:
1. You now have control over your sales results and financial success.

2. You'll have less anxiety over where you're going to get your next sale.
3. The number of sales opportunities will increase.
4. You will meet some interesting and great people.
5. You will feel and act like a real professional, because a real pro always prospects.

**P.S.** Without robust prospecting activity, you will soon be unemployed.

# FOLLOW-UP

## Use Follow-Up to Reinforce Every Bridge You Have Built

*"A good follow-through is just as important in management as in bowling, tennis or golf. Follow-through is the bridge between good planning and good results."* — *Anonymous*

**Premise:**

In the sales process, there are expected requests for information and service by clients and prospects. Customers, prospects and team members rely on your promises. The sales professional who succeeds leaves a clear trail of kept commitments and follow-through, while a sales amateur will promise everything but deliver very little of value.

Sales are not a one-dimensional process. While you might prefer being at the front end of the funnel where all the sales are made, you must begin and continue the prospecting follow-through and follow-up or you'll eventually find that you're burning bridges as quickly as you're trying to build them. Eighty-seven percent of customer inquiries are never followed up by sales professionals. Don't allow yourself to be relegated to a profile of mediocrity.

**Symptoms of Impending Disaster:**
- In your mind, someone else should do the follow-up with your clients and prospects.
- Clients and prospects have to repeatedly ask you to follow-up on what you agreed to do.
- Your follow-up list is long and growing longer by the day.
- Your sales manager has to remind you constantly of promises you have made to him or her, and where your progress stands.
- When clients and prospects ask you about a follow-up item, you make a new promise to follow-up, knowing it will be hard to keep.

**Story:**

Recently, we invested in a new car. After various test drives, reviewing various publications and talking to car aficionados regarding the new models, my wife and I made a selection. Now, where to buy it?

We placed three phone calls to three car dealers and asked for information and pricing.

One never called back.

One called and said he would mail the information to me that day – it never arrived.

The third told me he would have the material FedExed to me the very next day. It arrived and was followed up with a courteous phone call, clarifying all questions. Additionally, he promised to have the car delivered to my front door.

Who do you think got the order? Rob Smith of Sierra Leasing in Glendale, California and his assistant, Colleen, who drove the car three hours to deliver it to my front door. Now, that's follow-up! The very next month our son Matt called Rob and invested in a new car.

**Solutions:**

1. Consider carefully what you specifically agree to follow-up.
2. Before you agree or volunteer a promise, ask yourself first if this is a commitment you can and intend to keep.
3. It's better to be silent than to set up incorrect expectations.
4. Record every commitment you make to clients and prospects and repeat it back to them for clarification.
5. Immediately schedule a time when you will complete the commitment personally or delegate it, scheduling time to follow-up on that delegation.
   a. Ask the client or prospect to call you if their expectations are not met. You are always available.
   b. Check off your completed follow-ups – a win for you.
   c. Each day, review your follow-up commitments.
   d. Take pride in your reputation as being the follow-up king or queen.

## Results:

1.  When follow-up becomes a habit, you'll find you have more time and energy for focused sales activity.
2.  You will experience less stress because you won't be doing things twice, or looking over your shoulder to see who's coming to you for answers on your commitments.
3.  Your customer reliability zooms upward.
4.  When you're on equal ground with your competitors, your ability to keep commitments will put you on higher ground every time.
5.  With fewer loose ends, your clients and prospects will obviously say "Yes" more often and more quickly.

**P.S.** In sales, poor follow-up with your clients results in lack of client trust and loyalty, which leads quickly to poor sales ... it's a poor habit.

# STAYING ON COURSE

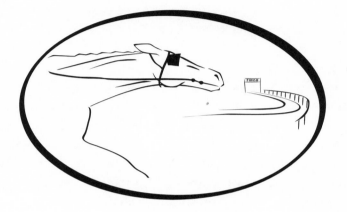

## CHANGE
### Change is the Breakfast of Champions

*"Change has a considerable psychological impact on the human mind.
To the fearful it is threatening because it means that things
may get worse. To the hopeful mind it is encouraging because things may
get better. To the confident it is inspiring because the challenge
exists to make things better." — King Whitney Jr.*

**Premise:**

Change will always bring winners and doers to the front of the line and send the losers packing. The horse-and-buggy manufacturer who thought he was in the buggy business forever is long since gone, while those in the buggy business who saw themselves as members of the transportation business adjusted with the changes and survived. They saw themselves as implementers of change. Seek new opportunity at all turns. Embrace change.

**Symptoms of Impending Disaster:**
- You resist change of any kind.
- You long for the good old days.
- Every time a new sales idea comes up, you can't help but immediately cite the many challenging problems associated with this new, insane change.
- When new plans or changes are announced, you find a way to involve your team members in trashing it.
- You're using your mind to think of the negative "why NOT reason" instead of the positive "WHY reasons."
- You are more and more rigid in your thinking.

**Story:**

One fall day, I was fishing in Silver Creek, Sun Valley Idaho, with my friend and guide, Dave Falting from Terry Ring's Silver Creek Outfitters. I noticed that another fisherman downstream from us was not enjoying our blue-ribbon day.

As the massive hatch would change, my good buddy and guide would stop, analyze the dead flies floating past us in the water, and have me tie on a new, appropriate fly. I was frustrated because this took time away from casting to those giant, rising rainbow trout. I just knew too many were getting away.

At the end of the day, when we walked down the bank, the other fisherman who had fished downstream approached us and confided that he had a very tough day and noticed that we were constantly netting another big catch. He sheepishly asked if we would share our success. Dave said, "We constantly changed our tools and ammunition. As the hatch changed, we changed in order to match the trout's appetite."

Our buddy downstream just kept casting the same old fly – he got a lot of exercise, but he didn't make the big catch. In sales, just like in fly-fishing, you have to change quickly as the conditions change.

## Solutions:

1. Accept that change is inevitable and constant.
2. Every day, look for new and better ways to do things.
3. Ask yourself the dumb questions: "Why am I doing it this way?" You might get a smart answer.
4. Periodically introduce change into your business and professional life, i.e., take a new route to work.
5. With each announcement of change, stop yourself for just two minutes to mentally explore all the positive opportunities that will come with this change.
6. Observe those successful pros around you and ask how they respond to change.

## Results:

1. You'll be exerting your energy in the right direction – toward change.
2. Clients will see you as a forward-thinking individual.
3. Your sales management team will see you as progressive and

include you in front-end discussions that lead to change.
4. You will marvel at your own solutions involving change – especially when you discover that they work!
5. Look forward to change. Court it, welcome it.

**P.S.** The sales consultant who first recognizes a paradigm shift and makes the appropriate change will win the next sale.

# FLEXIBILITY

## Your Flexibility is All Tied Up

*"Reasonable people adapt themselves to the world. Unreasonable people attempt to adapt the world to themselves."*
*– George Bernard Shaw*

**Premise:**

In a perfect world, everything happens according to the schedule – plane flights, building construction, traffic flow, teenagers home on time and, of course, clients and prospects keeping their appointments. However, clients and prospects will think nothing of asking you to change your carefully assembled schedule. Yes, the need to be flexible is a constant in life and in the sales profession.

**Symptoms of Impending Disaster:**

- You become irritated when your friends want to change the times for your social get-togethers.
- When clients and prospects cancel or reschedule your appointments, you start talking to yourself, i.e., "The nerve of that so-and-so."
- When asked to change a time or date, you'll occasionally tell a white lie in order to combat the schedule change.
- You don't offer to be flexible when asked by good, long-term clients or prospects.
- Your subconscious thinks being flexible is a sign of weakness.
- You think being flexible will encourage clients and prospects to abuse your time.
- You are known as Mr./Ms. Rigid.

**Story:**

In my business, clothing and grooming sends a loud message. I'm fortunate to have a friend named Tony Belmaggio who is a wonderful tailor and a great human being. One day I thanked him for such great personal treatment and service. With his big infectious Italian smile he replied, "Jack, it's because you're flexible and not demanding with me. For many of my clients, everything is ASAP. If it's OK with your schedule, you always let me adjust when I have over-demanding clients or circumstances beyond my control. You know – late fabric deliveries or client emergencies. So, on that rare occasion when you DO ask for something quickly, I immediately put you at the head of the line."

**Solutions:**
1. Observe others who are flexible and those who are inflexible and decide who you'd rather be around and do business with.
2. Accept that being flexible is a valuable asset for a professional sales competitor.
3. Always look at the possibilities if you are asked by a client or prospect to be flexible regarding your schedule or meetings.
4. If an opportunity to be flexible arises, stop and say to yourself, "I love being flexible." Mean it!
5. Keep a record of when you refused to be flexible and ask yourself, "Why didn't I take the opportunity to demonstrate my ability to help my clients and prospects and be flexible? Was I selfish? Was I inflexible?"

**Results:**
1. You will enjoy a reputation of being easy and affable in business dealings.
2. You will see more opportunities come your way because you've expanded the ways in which people can do business with you.
3. Flexibility is a two-way street and, as a result, clients and prospects remember that you were flexible when they needed it. Therefore, they will extend you flexibility when you need it.
4. If demanding and complex situations for clients come up and they need a dependable solution, they will turn to you because of your reputation for being flexible and adaptable.
5. In competitive situations, you will acquire new business from

clients and prospects who feel they owe you a favor because of your prior flexibility.

6. You might pick off a tough prospect who calls you in a pinch for help if you make changes to accommodate him.

7. By being a flexible person, you're open to more possible solutions.


**P.S.** While being flexible helps you in yoga, it gives you the extra card in the sales game – and more cards equals more chances to win.

# IMPULSIVE

## Why Impatient and Abrupt Salespeople Get Fired – and How You Can Avoid that Fate!

*"Fools rush in where angels fear to tread."*
*— Alexander Pope*

**Premise:**

Impulsive actions can attract attention and momentarily solve a problem on a short-term basis. While being proactive is a permanent step in achieving your goals, one must also beware of the danger of taking an impulsive action without carefully calculating the consequences.

Abrupt and impetuous actions can lead to a reputation for being hasty and shooting from the hip.

**Symptoms of Impending Disaster:**

- You make hasty decisions on major issues and your nickname is "Mr. or Ms. Hasty-Wasty."
- Your friends feel that you're abrupt, short-spoken and jump to conclusions in your social conversations.
- When discussing a solution for a client who has a problem, you immediately interrupt and rush to conclusions.
- You have no patience when discussing alternative solutions for your clients and prospects.
- In team meetings, you try to force the group to act quickly without due consideration.
- You secretly believe losers are overly patient and slow to act and, as a result, miss the chance to get on with things.
- You have to revisit and revise many hasty and poorly thought-out actions.

**Story:**

I've always made it clear to my team members that I'm committed to giving them timely, candid and honest advice when they receive offers from competitors. At Wood Logan, a division of John Hancock, we select and train the best and, therefore, it never surprises me when the competitors try to steal our sales champions. It's a true compliment.

In 1998, Chuck came to see me one evening with a job offer that he'd just received from one of our major, fine competitors. Chuck was a good team member with an excellent family, and I wasn't surprised at the large, six-figure earnings offer. As we sat on the sofa at the Hotel del Coronado, Chuck laid out the attractive terms he'd been offered. After listening carefully, I advised Chuck that he had to talk to them to get more facts. Additionally, he received advice from John Egbert, our national sales manager. John also told him to make sure he got the facts right, because John personally cared about his sales team and their families and wanted them to make the right decisions.

The very next day, I got a call from Chuck – he had made a decision to accept the offer from the other firm.

Two years later, the sales division he'd entered for this competitor was discontinued. Recently, Chuck confided in me that it was a good short-term decision, but perhaps a bit hasty and very poor long-term decision for his career. It was a classic example of the truism: The grass appeared greener in that other pasture.

**Solutions:**
1. Slow down on your major decisions.
2. Get input on serious decisions.
3. When you have the urge to act abruptly, count to 10 and ask, "Have I truly gathered every fact I need for this decision?"
4. With your team members, encourage a full discussion of major issues before any decision.
5. Let your clients and prospects see you as a careful and deliberate decision maker.
6. Ask for input on those serious decisions.
7. Take pride in being a careful, premeditated decision maker.
8. Your new mantra is: "Patience spoken and practiced here."

**Results:**

1. Your sales management team will give your ideas greater consideration because they know you've deliberated over these ideas before presenting them.
2. In group meetings, you will make a greater contribution because of your perception as a deliberate decision maker.
3. Socially, your friends will encourage you to share your points of view because they value the quality time you invest in decisions.
4. Your clients and prospects will accept your proposals and solutions as being well thought out.
5. You will make fewer mistakes.
6. You will have to reverse few, if any, of your decisions.

**P.S.** Retired Marine Colonel James Manley uses the following rule: SEDA – Sense, Evaluate, Decide & Act.

# PROCRASTINATION

## How to Conquer Procrastination and Slay the Demons of Delay

*"Procrastination is the thief of time." – Edward Young*

**Premise:**

As a leader, you are expected to act on a timely basis with no excuses. Endless delays and overanalysis of decisions results in serious paralysis. A stagnant business, a struggling sales territory, a confused mind – these are the properties of an unfocused sales professional. While we all make mistakes by our actions, it's far better to act than to live your life in the parking lot. By procrastinating, you're avoiding a decision to act now. And by delaying, you are only floating and not swimming forward. One thing done well beats 10 things half-done.

**Symptoms of Impending Disaster:**
- You find yourself always saying, "Let's think about it."
- You frequently say, "Let me get back to you with an answer tomorrow."
- You seem to have numerous decisions in front of you every morning that have carried over from days before.
- Your activity list is like good wine – well aged.
- You change your mind frequently on key issues.
- Just putting things off seems easier than taking action.
- Your sales team members and the support sales team are always waiting on you.
- Each day, you waste time rethinking your previous decisions.
- Your boss isn't sure where your mind is on critical company issues. Neither are you.

**Story:**

While managing IBM's Washington D.C. office, I had a potential superstar named Charlie. He possessed all the tools for a successful sales career. However, he was missing one key ingredient: Charlie couldn't make a decision without hours of deliberation. It was easier to delay than to put it on the line. It seemed like a daily ritual with Charlie. It was delay after delay. For Charlie, it was nearly fatal.

Finally, I had to give Charlie the ultimatum – start making decisions or I would have to make the decision to replace him with a person of action. Now, as I said, Charlie was smart and ambitious. He got the message and the jolt caused him to put his procrastination disease on hold. We both won. Charlie got on with the business of selling and I had more time to invest in other team solutions.

### Solutions:
1. Look for the root of your procrastination on certain items. Are you unsure? Do you not have enough information? Are you bored with it? Are you afraid to make a mistake?
2. Do not overanalyze every situation.
3. Get the facts straight and then have the courage to take immediate action.
4. Pride yourself in not having a backlog of aging key decisions that need to be made now.
5. When you find yourself swaying back-and-forth or simply avoiding major decisions, take charge.
6. Consider using the old Ben Franklin T-Account Chart, putting the pluses on one side and minuses on the other, and making a decision from there.
7. Check-in with your sales manager and administrative support team and ask if there are any decisions you need to make at this time.
8. Recognize that we all make mistakes. In his book, *Think and Grow Rich*, Napoleon Hill states that, "True leaders are quick to make decisions and careful to change their minds."
9. Don't fear making a mistake.

**Results:**
1. You will find yourself free for new opportunities.
2. You will have a reputation as a person of action.
3. In times of need, clients, team members and your sales management team will turn to you as a timely and decisive decision maker.
4. You will make more decisions faster and, therefore, accomplish more.
5. You will make more productive use of your valuable time.
6. You will have more success and, at the same time, will make mistakes. As a result, you will learn from your actions.
7. Tomorrow will no longer be the busiest day of the week.

**P.S.** Put your procrastination habit in the trash can.

# DISTRACTIONS

## Distractions Have Detoured You from the Highway of Success

*"You will never get the brass ring for sales success if you allow your*
*personal activity and relationships to control your business day."*
*— Jack Perry*

**Premise:**

By nature, most people are easily distracted. With the various roles we all play, distraction can become a powerful disrupting force. You might play one or more of these roles every day: friend, spouse, Little League coach, charity volunteer or professional sales consultant. With each role, you must choose when and how to allocate your time, energy and resources. To succeed in each role, you must remain completely focused and, therefore, reduce interruptions and distractions to a minimum.

**Symptoms of Impending Disaster:**
- You frequently receive calls at your workplace from family members about social activities.
- You take daily calls from friends rehashing the recent results of your favorite professional sport teams.
- You are spending meaningful time during your business day doing personal errands for yourself and your family.
- Your "To Do" list is jammed full of personal activities.
- The receptionist knows your family and friends by first name because they call so often.
- You have left sales meetings to take a personal, non-urgent phone call.
- You are frequently multitasking.
- It is hard for you to focus because of frequent interruptions.
- You have a growing stack of unfinished projects.
- You're frequently late to social events because of the disruptions during your day.
- You think distractions are just a normal way of running a business.

**Story:**

During my college days at UCLA, I had a job as a "hasher" (a meal serving/dish clean up role) at the Theta sorority house in West L.A. Yes, washing dishes three times a day, five days a week, $10 in cash, eating like a king and always being sent home on the weekends with food in my pockets from the house manager "Mrs. L," was a good life. And, of course, there were girls – yes, these very attractive young ladies were certainly a distraction.

Mrs. L. was not a fool, and she had rules relating to the hashers' conduct while serving her sorority girls. One of our hasher buddies was a great, tall fellow with a nasty habit of peeking at the girls over the top of the dining room door while they were eating their meals. Finally, Mrs. L. had enough of the hasher's distractions and put an end to it: she fired him.

The moral of the story: Keep your eye on your responsibilities and not the distractions, as tempting as they might be.

**Solutions:**

1. Accept the fact that you're being distracted and choose to stop it.
2. Build a defense plan against distractions.
   a. Make family agreements against interruptions.
   b. Schedule your errands during non-selling time.
   c. Delegate whenever possible.
   d. Get your family involved in helping you when they are available.
   e. Make your personal calls quick and to the point.
3. Choose to focus on quality time and not quantity time in your personal relationships.
4. When you start something, make a commitment to finish it. Do not allow yourself to be interrupted.
5. Ask for an accountability check from your sales management team.
6. Manage your social life in non-selling hours.

**Results:**
1. You will have a better focus.
2. You'll waste less time because you won't be starting and stopping and starting the same project in a single day.
3. You'll have better utilization of your energy by focusing on one project at a time.
4. You will enjoy increased peace of mind.
5. You'll have more time to invest in the sales process, therefore earning better results.

**P.S.** Don't let distractions destroy your sales career opportunity.

# SPENDTHRIFT

## How to Escape From the Prison of Debt

*"I've been rich and I've been poor. Rich is better."*
*— Sophie Tucker*

**Premise:**

There's a significant difference between your needs and your wants. We all must make deliberate choices between the two each day, in all aspects of our lives. Deciding your wants vs. your needs has a huge impact on your financial health. When your mind is crowded with your financial challenges, how can you expect to focus on a successful sales career? As we all know, it's not what you make, it's what you keep. Living beyond your means is an automatic entry into the poverty club.

**Symptoms of Impending Disaster:**

* Your financial issues are dragging you off course.
* Lately, you've been slow paying your bills.
* You could join the circus with your checkbook juggling act.
* You're spending more time and effort moving your money around and focusing on the deficits in your accounts than you are on earning more money.
* It seems the phrases "Keeping up with the Joneses" and "Living beyond your means" were created with you in mind.
* You're nervous during your presentations because of the need to close the sale in order to reduce your personal checking account's deficits.
* You have chosen not to invest in yourself, because your personal spending habits have eaten up all your investment dollars.
* You're wasting precious time worrying about your finances.
* You can't say "no" to social outings that are beyond your financial means.

**Story:**

When our oldest son, Wade, was starting his new career after college graduation, he was showing me his expertise with a new software program, Quicken. Much to his surprise, his credit card accounts accidentally appeared on his computer screen. Let me interject that we never gave our sons large amounts of spending money during their college days. During his late junior and senior years in school, Wade had decided to take advantage of the seductive offers from credit card companies directed at college students. Now, at last he could enjoy entertaining his friends in style. Oh, boy.

After a rather meaningful father-and-son conversation, he voluntarily cut his credit cards in half and sent them home to his mother. When Judy received the cards, she fanned them out as one would with a hand of cards, and placed them in a frame with a heads-up statement below: A Losing Hand. That framed reminder hangs in Wade's office today and credit card debt has no place in his family's life.

**Solutions:**

1. Take a spending audit to identify where you are financially at the present.
2. Create a financial audit of your assets, liabilities, net worth, savings and retirement accounts.
3. Consider hiring a financial advisor.
4. Develop a specific budget and live by it.
5. Always pay yourself first. Before you do anything else, write a check to your savings or investment account every month, and then decide how you're going to spend the rest of your money.
6. Each month, track actual vs. budgeted expenditures.
7. Take pride in living on less money than you make.
8. Learn to analyze and come face-to-face with your wants vs. your needs.

**Results:**
1.  Your mind will be free to focus on your sales career opportunity.
2.  Now, your money will be invested wisely.
3.  Your checkbook will wear a happy face.
4.  You will experience less emotional stress.
5.  You'll have more energy to use productively in the sales process.
6.  Your money will now work for you and not your creditors.
7.  No more embarrassing calls from credit card companies regarding delinquent bills.

**P.S.** Living successfully within your means is a very personal choice.

# RESOURCEFUL

## How to Develop a Resourceful Mind-set

*"Difficulties are things that show what men are." — Epicetetus*

**Premise:**

In most cases, clients and prospects don't just want a product or service source. Clients want a resource center, a reliable source for pertinent information to help them with all their solutions. Some requests for solutions are easy; some requests require the full resources of the firm. The sales professional must know how to access the many resources available.

**Symptoms of Impending Disaster:**

- Your view of your sales career is very narrow. It's all about your product and service.
- You frequently tell clients and prospects that you cannot help them when they request information that is unrelated to your product or service.
- You do not have a network of professionals who can help you solve client and prospect needs.
- In your firm, others do not seek you out for solutions.
- Management teams do not seek your help because of your limited resources.
- You don't expand your basic knowledge through reading, study and seminars.
- Your outside reading program consists of the sports page.

**Story:**

Eric Neff has developed into a marvelous sales professional for Manulife Wood Logan. Early in Eric's career there, he decided he didn't want to be a commodity – just another wholesaler delivering literature. Eric chose to position himself as a reliable resource for his clients and prospects. With this mission statement in mind, he told his clients and prospects that he was available as a resource to help them solve their challenges, regardless of the fact that it might not relate directly to his product or service.

As a result, Eric significantly increased his value in the eyes of his clients and prospects, while rapidly expanding his base of knowledge. Mr. Resourceful has used his knowledge base and availability as a tool to build a very rewarding sales business. Eric is a reliable resource to his clients and prospects.

### Solutions:

1. Recognize the fact that you are but a commodity and must separate yourself from the crowd.
2. Position yourself as a resource.
3. Be a valuable source of information for others.
4. Build a network for source information.
5. Tell your clients and prospects that they can feel comfortable calling you about other needs.
6. Have a "Can Do" attitude.
7. Ask your clients and prospects what their biggest challenges are, and find ways to help them specifically with those issues.
8. Maintain an up-to-date client relationship management system.
9. Tell your clients and prospects that you are different from your competitors and you will demonstrate as much with your added value.
10. Help your clients and prospects keep their promises.

### Results:

1. Clients and prospects will seek you out for help.
2. Your pertinent knowledge for clients and prospects will expand.
3. Your team members will come to you for help.
4. Your value will grow in the eyes of your clients and prospects.
5. The sales management team will seek your advice.
6. When it's a close call, your clients and prospects will award you the business.

**P.S.** Establish yourself as the ultimate resource for your clients and prospects.

# PRIDE

## Show Pride in Your Profession

*"Keep true, never be ashamed of doing right; decide on what
you think is right and stick to it." — George Eliot*

**Premise:**

To be successful in business, you must love what you do and respect your chosen profession. It is natural to look for excuses when things don't go as planned and cast your eye at another seemingly more attractive and respected career. If you or your family look upon the sales function as a necessary evil for business and a job that carries little respect from your fellow man, you need to make an immediate course correction in your career.

Make sure you are mentally ready for the opportunity to excel as a sales professional, or make the decision to change careers. Sales is not for the timid at heart or the uncommitted. That's why the true sales professionals are well rewarded in terms of satisfaction in providing client solutions and income that comes with sales success. When asked in a social gathering, you must be prepared to say that you're proud to be a sales professional.

**Symptoms of Impending Disaster:**

* You have negative thoughts about the image of a salesperson.
* Your family and friends knock sales as a profession and you don't reply.
* You don't appreciate the role the sales team plays in a successful business.
* None of your heroes are salespeople.
* You disguise the sales role with vague or esoteric definitions in order to avoid being viewed as a lowly sales person.
* Your library is not stocked with any books on selling skills.
* You subconsciously think selling is arm twisting.
* When asked, "What is it you do?" you quickly mumble, "I'm in sales," and change the subject.

- You don't ever push hard to get the prospect to accept the solution you believe in because you think that is selling, which you don't respect.

**Story:**

When I was in the financial services industry as a branch manager for what is now Smith Barney, one of my financial advisors told me during his performance review that he wasn't a broker or advisor – he was a "client service specialist."

I sat back and said, "That's news to me. Last time I checked, your opportunity here is to go out every day hunting for people who have a problem/challenge with their investment portfolio, then offer appropriate solutions to help them achieve their financial goals. Yes, we always need Client Service Specialists. But you are being paid to be the Rainmaker."

Shortly thereafter, the broker made a career change out of selling.

**Solutions:**

1. Let's get real here. Accept your opportunity as a professional sales advisor – one of the finest professions in business with boundless opportunity – or go out and get another job.
2. Take great pride in solving problems for clients and prospects and creating new business for your firm.
3. Look at yourself in the mirror each morning and tell yourself, "I loooove being a sales professional!"
4. You must believe in the value you deliver to your clients and prospects by probing, verifying and presenting solutions for their needs.
5. Don't associate with sales people who express doubt regarding the value of the sales professions.
6. Educate your family regarding the value of sales in our society.
7. Make a point of sharing stories with family and friends regarding solutions you've provided in helping clients and prospects.

8. Read and study books and articles that have to do with successful sales professionals.

**Results:**
1. No more wasted time, energy and emotions on negative thoughts regarding the value of selling in our society.
2. You will swell with pride when you clearly tell people that you are a professional salesperson.
3. Your entire commitment to the sales process changes and you will push for decisions that are good for clients and prospects.
4. You will be more effective in getting clients and prospects to accept solutions to their needs.
5. You will help the new, younger sales team members make the same commitment you did or change careers.

**P.S.** Nothing happens in business until a sale takes place. You must be the first to be sold on the concept.

# REJECTION

### Reject Rejection or You Will be Rejected from Your Career

*"Don't waste yourself in rejection, nor bark against the bad, but chant the beauty of the good." — Ralph Waldo Emerson*

## Premise:

You control the gate for information that enters your mind. When you receive a potential rejection from a client or prospect, you can see it for what it is, or allow it to let the air out of your tires. Rejection only comes to live where it's given a room. It's up to you to decide whether you're going to reject rejection or give it a permanent bedroom in your mind.

## Symptoms of Impending Disaster:

- You don't understand that, in the sales process, clients and prospects will occasionally try to reject your ideas.
- You're taking sales rejections personally. You have to ensure that you will separate the idea from you the individual when the potential rejection is thrown your way.
- You have a very low closing ratio.
- Your sales manager points out that you have too few new accounts.
- In a sales presentation, you're quitting after you get the first rejection.
- People can see rejection in your eyes and in your body language.
- In every sale, someone gets sold, but you notice that YOU are frequently the one agreeing with the client or prospect.
- Rejection Depression has you in its grip.

## Story:

My first time at bat in the sales arena was with Occidental Life Insurance in Pasadena, California, right out of the U.S. Army, where I had served as an artillery officer. Training in those days was real time – "Here's the rate book, here's the desk, the brochures are in the cabinet, and the phone directories are on the shelf. Good luck." Fortunately, I had a very fine producing sales manager who cared about people and gave us as much time as he could, considering the fact that he was also a producer.

After finally over preparing and making those first phone calls, I started to experience sales rejection. I was allowing unknown people who were faceless to me to reject me as well as my ideas. Soon, my activity dropped and, boy, I could shuffle those prospect cards like a Las Vegas blackjack dealer. They were worn out.

Finally one day my manager, Len, took me aside to review my purpose in sales, and my purpose in life insurance to help me understand the process. It became very clear that I did not fully understand that I was not being rejected but was, in fact, not arriving at the right time at the right place with solutions. Len reminded me that sales is a numbers game, and that for every "No" I received (a.k.a. rejection), I was that much closer to a sale. He pointed out that if, for example, it took 50 contacts to get 10 appointments to see five people, I'd get three sales. He recommended that I keep call records so that I could actually see myself getting closer to one of those 10 appointments and that much closer to those three precious sales.

Yes, counting put the process into perspective. I soon learned that all sales are numbers games and my fear of rejection dissipated.

## Solutions:

1. It is first important that you take an inventory of your mind and make sure that you've not established a bedroom there for the Rejection Disease.
2. In all sales, understand that you're a worthwhile person with worthwhile ideas and that the prospect cannot possibly reject you. He can only reject your ideas at that moment in time.
3. Rejection is part of the sales process. Use it to your advantage.
4. In role-play, have people try to reject your ideas and, in the process, you.

5. Flash a big smile when a client or prospect gives you the rejection treatment.

6. Set up a mental button in your mind labeled "EJECT." When rejection starts to creep into your mind, immediately press that button and see rejection jettisoned like James Bond sailing out of harm's way.

7. Remind yourself that when a prospect says "No," he means "Maybe." Find the pain and offer a solution he needs.

**Results:**

1. You are ready to hear and redirect rejection attempts.

2. As part of your persistency habit, clients and prospects will perceive your handling of rejection with respect.

3. No more energy will be drained or confidence lost from Rejection Depression.

4. You will notice that you're not quitting after the first or second "No," but working until that "No becomes a "Yes."

5. You'll start to increase your closing success ratio.

**P.S.** When you're not letting rejection live in your house, you're letting success have more space in your mind and life.

# MONEY

## How to Make Money Your Friend and Ally

*"No one would remember the Good Samaritan if he'd only had good intentions. He had money as well."* — Margaret Thatcher

## Premise:

I never found and trained a sales consultant or sales coach, or sales manager who didn't have the desire to make a lot of money. Money is not good or bad; we all need it. And, clients and prospects want to deal with successful people who are earning money in their profession. Remember, you don't use money to show off, but rather find ways to put money to a good use to help family, communities, schools, charity, your retirement and more. Without money – and more of it – our whole economic system would take a nosedive and negatively impact the health and freedoms we enjoy that only affluence can underwrite.

Money is also a way of keeping your personal score. What would golf or football be like if you didn't keep score?

## Symptoms of Impending Disaster:

- You always find fault with sales leaders and money-earning leaders by attacking their chosen habits and lifestyles.
- You rationalize that money is not important and your seven-year-old car with 150,000 miles on the odometer is just fine.
- While attacking the lifestyle of successful sales people, you are not living the lifestyle of your dreams.
- You complain about the compensation plan even though you don't choose to max out the plan.
- You ask for more expense money even though you're not producing more sales.
- You secretly believe people with lots of money could not be happy or be fulfilled.

## Story:

While interviewing at UCLA in the 1960s for new sales team

members at IBM, I encountered what appeared to be a potential superstar. He was articulate, well-groomed, had great presence, and was very likeable. When I came to the subject of money, he said it really wasn't important and didn't mean anything in his life. I told him that in many careers money was not an issue, and you should never pursue a career just for money. One should find something in life that one loves and go out and do it. I then leaned forward, looked him in the eye, and said, "But, money does have a meaningful place in successful sales careers. When it becomes important to you for good and valid reasons, come and see me."

## Solutions:
1. Have a plan for earning the money.
2. Set specific income goals. Write them down and look at them daily.
3. Establish a plan for the use of your money.
4. Use the money for the good of your family, community, charity, your country and your retirement plan.
5. Don't be greedy.
6. When you start to knock the rich, switch gears and ask how you can get there and then use the trappings of success (money) for the right reasons.

## Results:
1. Your options change when you have money. You have more opportunities.
2. People want to do business with successful people.
3. You will look and act more prosperous and, thus, attract more clients and prospects.
4. You will help people, charities and communities as you proceed on your journey.
5. Your sales will go up; the money in your investment and retirement accounts is a by-product.

**P.S.** Drive your sales higher, let the cash register ring, and put your money to good use.

## COMPETITIVE

### You've Lost That Competitive Feeling

*"I don't meet competition. I crush it."*
*— Charles Revson*

**Premise:**

Competition makes competitive sales professionals better – they work harder and smarter. Yes, to be a successful sales professional, you DO want to win. You have to want big sales numbers and big successes and that does mean that you have to get out there and win business. You must beat a competitor for the business. Being competitive in business requires that same internal fire as being competitive in athletics. You have to hate to lose and be willing to pay the price in order to enjoy the spoils of victory: opportunities, respect and money. And, in the process, you'll avoid that deep pain of defeat.

**Symptoms of Impending Disaster:**

- You choose not to pay the price for sales success.
- You're becoming more and more comfortable being in the bottom sales quartile.
- You are quick to find fault with the company's sales volume leaders.
- You find it easier to slip into the crowd and avoid the energy and commitment of being competitive.
- You feel that the sales leaders probably don't enjoy life the way you do.
- You're afraid of failure. If you don't try, you can't fail.
- It doesn't upset you when you lose a big account.
- You dislike making presentations with your competitors in the room.
- You don't actively call on your toughest prospects.
- You become apprehensive when told you'll be competing next

week at the sales meeting in a sales presentation contest.
- You hate sales contests.

**Story:**

In Boulder City, Nevada, a combination baseball/track meet was held to determine league championship. It was my senior year of high school in Blythe, California and we needed one more point to win the meet. It looked as if we were doomed because we didn't have an entry for the last event. My friend, Clancy Osborne, though an all-around athlete in superb condition, was not a track man, he was there officially to play baseball for Blythe. Knowing we needed a point, Clancy went to our coach, Tom Woodburn, and volunteered to enter the mile run, though he had never competed in that event. As the group of runners dashed toward the finish, Clancy was in the center of the track and running neck-and-neck with the projected winner. In a last ditch move, Clancy went airborne and threw himself ahead of the competitor – head-long in flight onto a cinder track – and into a slide and tumble that left him bruised and bloody. He was triumphant, though. He'd scored the point we needed. Clancy, "Mr. Competitive," went on to Arizona State, then played linebacker for the Los Angeles Rams.

**Solutions:**
1. Make a decision that being competitive is the real you. It doesn't mean that you have to punch someone in the nose, but it does mean that you have to push yourself harder and farther than you ever have before.
2. Every morning and every evening, take one of your goals, close your eyes and visualize the joy in accomplishing it. See it happening.
3. You must purposely move out of your comfort zone.
4. Never allow yourself to accept a defeat as permanent in nature.
5. Have that competitive look, feel and air about you.
6. Ask the sales management team for the toughest prospects.

7.  When sales contests are announced, immediately implement plans to be a winner.
8.  Never, never, never quit.

**Results:**
1.  Being competitive will bring out your very best performance.
2.  Your energy will be focused on the positive aspects of being competitive.
3.  You will start shooting for the stars and accomplish more of everything.
4.  You will not take "no" for an answer.
5.  You will convert some of those tough prospects into clients.
6.  You will actually enjoy looking at yourself in the mirror.
7.  You will win more often.

**P.S.** Everyone loves a competitor.

# PERSISTENCE

## How to Prepare for the Marathon

*"Nothing in this world can take the place of persistence. Talent will not; nothing is more common than unsuccessful people with talent. Genius will not; unrewarded genius is almost a proverb. Education will not; the world is full of educated derelicts. Persistence and determination alone are omnipotent. The slogan "press on" has solved and always will solve the problems of the human race." — Calvin Coolidge*

**Premise:**

Life is not a 100-yard dash. It's a marathon. Persistency in the sales profession is far more important than talent. Talented people can shine brightly on a project, get fully involved and create results, but the project will fail if they don't have the persistency to stay after it when challenges present themselves along the way. Persistency in sales means coming back to clients and prospects again and again. You don't quit.

**Symptoms of Impending Disaster:**

- You notice that you're usually quitting on that first call if it doesn't go your way.
- Tough projects always seem as if they're requiring entirely too much effort on your part.
- You have a history of giving up when the going gets tough.
- You don't probe when a client or prospect gives you the deadly "No."
- While you have a relatively high sales call count, your closing ratio is very low. Bad sign.
- In many projects, you decide that being mediocre is good enough and that you don't need to persist to a higher level of accomplishment.
- Some weeks and months your activity is sky-high while similar time frames see it at a rock-bottom low.

- Your lack of persistency is affecting your attitude and daily feelings.
- You don't know what focused commitment looks like or feels like anymore.

**Story:**

Wood Logan has always been one of the premier marketing companies in the financial services industry. As a result, they've always been demanding and particular in their selection of team members. In December 1990, Tony Pappas, a successful insurance and investment specialist in the Michigan area, decided he wanted to join Wood Logan and asked for a job even though he didn't fit their precise model for the opportunity. Bob Cassato, the national sales manager, now president of the firm, thanked him and said they were looking for someone who had "in-territory" contacts. Tony thanked Bob, but Wood Logan didn't know Tony.

Tony felt the opportunity was worth fighting for, and his campaign began.

- He had five high-ranking company presidents of broker/dealers write letters of recommendation.
- As a member of the parish council, he asked his parish priest to write a letter of recommendation.
- He sent letters to the president and chairman of the Wood Logan board, and the national sales manager giving them 100 reasons why they should hire him.
- And, every other week, he'd send each of them a new sales idea. Tony's persistency dance continued until March. Finally, the Wood Logan Chairman, Doug Wood, called Tony at home on Friday and said, "You're hired." Tony's persistency had won the day. To this day, Tony continues to be an immense success.

**Solutions:**

1. Accept that to succeed in sales, you must love to be persistent.
2. Pride yourself in being a persistent sales professional.

3. Analyze those situations where you quit and did not persist. What stopped you?
4. When you hit roadblocks, back off, reload and try again.
5. Never accept defeat, only experience minor setbacks.
6. Always probe deeper when you get the hated "No."
7. Tell clients and prospects that if your current solution does not work for them, you will continue to offer other solutions in the future.

**Results:**
1. Ultimately, you'll begin turning many a "no" into a "yes" because you're helping clients solve problems they reveal to you due to your persistency.
2. You will develop long-time relationships because your clients admire your persistency.
3. Your competition will fear you.
4. You will convert more prospects to clients.
5. You will get business by default because your competitors will have given up.
6. While you might not get the current sale, you will get the future sale.

**P.S.** In my own life, I've experienced setbacks, not defeats. As a result, I came up with my mantra several years ago: "They don't make bullets big enough to kill me." Keep coming back for more and, sooner than later, you'll find yourself the only player left in the game.

# PERSEVERANCE

## Discover the Power of Perseverance

*"I can summarize the lessons of my life in seven words — Never give in; never, never give in." — Winston Churchill*

**Premise:**

Ordinary people who choose to do extraordinary activities produce success. Look around you at those who are succeeding and recognize this: They don't have a magic formula. They understand that they must persist with an unyielding determination in order to achieve their goals, regardless of the circumstances or hardships. All things being equal, perseverance will be the leading force in defeating all of your obstacles.

**Symptoms of Impending Disaster:**
- When it's hot and you're tired, you call it a day even though it's only 3:00 in the afternoon.
- In school, if the class proved to be demanding you dropped it.
- When a major prospect has delivered you the big "NO" two or three times, you just quit calling.
- When your client or prospect has a problem that requires extensive research, you just quit.
- Your parents didn't make you finish what you started. Blame it on them.
- You don't complete the tough projects.
- When role-playing with the rookies, you're too easy on them.
- You hang around with a crowd that gives up easily. They like to coast. It's easier than pedaling uphill.
- You're traditionally low on the totem pole when completing company directives.

**Story:**

In 1779, the King of France gave John Paul Jones the command of an aging cargo ship. It was refitted, repaired and given the name,

*Bonne Homme Richard*. With four other ships, Jones set sail on Aug 14, 1779 to raid the English shipping fleet.

On Sept 23, 1779, his ship engaged the British ship, *The HMS Serapis*, just off the English coast. Jones' ship, *The Bonne Homme Richard*, took a broadside hit in the initial exchange, losing firepower and many of its gunners.

The commander of the *Serapis*, Richard Pearson, called out to Jones and asked if he would surrender. Hanging to the mast by one arm, Jones issued the immortal reply, "I have not yet begun to fight." Bloody battle continued and Jones and his crew fought tenaciously as their ship began to sink. As the fierce battle continued, British Commander Pearson finally withdrew his colors and surrendered. And just in time – the next day, the *Bonne Homme* sank.

Jones took command of the British ship and sailed off. Jones persevered and prevailed.

## Solutions:

1. Develop an attitude that when the going gets tough, you keep going.
2. Always finish what you started.
3. When you feel like quitting, examine your feelings and turn them around.
4. Build role models around you of people who persevere.
5. When presented with what you believe is a tough assignment, break it into small steps.
6. Push your own personal potential.
7. Teach a class to the rookies on perseverance.

## Results:

1. You will have a reputation for being the master of perseverance.
2. Clients and prospects know that when they don't accept one of your solutions, you will soon be back with another solution.
3. You will be given tough assignments because they know you will persevere.
4. You will experience less management supervision because they

    know you'll complete your projects.
5. You will wear down the competition.
6. You will increase your percentage of success on company targets.
7. You will find yourself associating with other persevering winners.
8. You will tap into more of your potential and experience personal satisfaction.

**P.S.** As you have often heard before, "When the going gets tough, the tough get going."

# HUNGRY

## Harness the Power of Hunger to Achieve Maximum Success

*"Your motivation? Your motivation is your pay packet on Friday.
Now get on with it." – Noel Coward*

**Premise:**

Being hungry in sales is an intangible, driving force based on a personal need, whether it is financial, pride, ego, job retention, competitiveness, or need for recognition. Imagine what you would do for food and water if you were forced to live without it for several days? Truly hungry people will go to great lengths to survive. Being hungry evokes from within an extra power and superior resolve. That same hunger should apply to your sales opportunity. When you are truly hungry to get the sale – for whatever your reason – your intensity turns up to maximum output level. You can see it in your eyes and in your actions.

**Symptoms of Impending Disaster:**
- You don't have any really big goals anymore.
- Being mediocre is just fine with you.
- You have allowed some big sales opportunities to slip away because you didn't have a burning desire to win.
- When the sales manager offers you a big potential client but warns you regarding the extra effort and challenges needed for success, you respond with, "I'll pass on this one."
- You can't remember when you were last fired up, over-the-top hungry about closing a specific prospect.
- A fatter commission check is not important to you.

**Story:**

While managing the western region for Wood Logan, a division of John Hancock, I frequently stressed the fact that your sales figures will rocket upward if you are hungry. Harold, one of my young team members, just wasn't hungry. He talked a good game, but the first inning was the final inning. He had inherited money and just didn't have any fire in his belly.

Because I cared about this young man and thought he had true sales potential, I arranged a one-on-one meeting with him. I said, "Harold, let's assume that you're in your office and I'm in my car driving by that charming Cape Cod that you and Maria have just bought. I notice smoke and leaping flames. I slam on the brakes, flip open my cell phone and call you immediately. 'Harold! Your house is on fire! You've got to get over there!'" Missing the point, Harold just looked at me. "Don't you see? You'd be amazed at what you could and would do if you had to!"

You see, if you're not hungry, you're not motivated to make the extra effort. You make no effort to improve yourself, your activity or your sales numbers. It's amazing what you can do when you absolutely must, when you have – excuse the pun – a burning desire.

## Solutions:

1. Question your motives for your sales success. How hungry are you?
2. Resolve to pay the price to blow through your activity numbers.
3. Set up personal future events that make it very important for you to succeed – dinner with a spouse, a meaningful gift to a charity, earning a specific amount of money in order to fund your child's college education.
4. Approach your biggest prospects with a tagline from Apollo 13, "Failure is not an option."
5. Aim to be recognized as a sales professional on a mission.
6. Always set higher standards and goals.

## Results:

1. When you're hungry, there's no limit to what you can accomplish in all phases of your life.
2. You will be amazed at what you can accomplish in sales in a single week with your new mantra, "I am HUNGRY!!"
3. You won't accept lame excuses anymore from clients and prospects.

4. Your competition will see the fire in your eyes and feel the heat from your intensity.
5. Your teammates and sales managers will ask you what got into your tank.
6. You will be a model to show both the tired old sales hacks and the new self-proclaimed hungry tigers.

**P.S.** To be a successful sales professional, you must adopt a hungry-hunter mentality and your desired results will be your trophy.

# APPENDIX

## PERSONAL SALES SKILL AUDIT

**1 = Never, 2 = Rarely, 3 = Sometimes,
4 = Most of the time, 5 = All of the time**

**Your candid answers will help you focus your energy and resources on improved results.**

**Your questions are as follows:**

**Section A – Mind-Set**

1 – When I go into work each morning, I remind myself
   to act like and think with an **ownership mind-set** . . . .1  2  3  4  5

2 – I keep my **commitments** . . . . . . . . . . . . . . . . . . . . . . . . .1  2  3  4  5

3 – Overall, I have a positive **attitude** . . . . . . . . . . . . . . . .1  2  3  4  5

4 – I consider the **integrity** of an issue before deciding
   on an action . . . . . . . . . . . . . . . . . . . . . . . . . . . . . . . . . .1  2  3  4  5

5 – I am **loyal** to my company and my clients . . . . . . . . . . .1  2  3  4  5

6 – I am recognized for **trusting** others . . . . . . . . . . . . . . . .1  2  3  4  5

**Section B – Direction**

7 – I read and update my **mission statement** regularly . . . .1  2  3  4  5

8 – I make, act on, and achieve my **goals** . . . . . . . . . . . . . .1  2  3  4  5

9 – I'm a consistent **planner** of activities throughout my day . .1  2  3  4  5

**Section C – In-Person First Impressions**

10 – I pay attention to the details of my **appearance** . . . . .1  2  3  4  5

11 – Generally, I'm considered a **likeable** person . . . . . . . .1  2  3  4  5

12 – People never doubt my **authenticity** . . . . . . . . . . . . . .1  2  3  4  5

13 – In all business and social settings, my **etiquette**
   is top-notch . . . . . . . . . . . . . . . . . . . . . . . . . . . . . . . . . .1  2  3  4  5

14 – I have a strong and positive **reputation** . . . . . . . . . . . .1  2  3  4  5

## Section D – Communication

15 – People say I have great **presence** . . . . . . . . . . . . . . . . .1   2   3   4   5

16 – I work on perfecting my **nonverbal** skills . . . . . . . . . .1   2   3   4   5

17 – I'm an **enthusiastic** person . . . . . . . . . . . . . . . . . . . .1   2   3   4   5

18 – I regularly **practice** my presentations . . . . . . . . . . . .1   2   3   4   5

19 – I'm constantly honing and improving my
     **questioning** skills . . . . . . . . . . . . . . . . . . . . . . . . . . . . .1   2   3   4   5

20 – I consciously work on my **listening** skills . . . . . . . . . .1   2   3   4   5

21 – I'm able to control my urge to be a **"motormouth"**
     in sales presentations . . . . . . . . . . . . . . . . . . . . . . . . .1   2   3   4   5

22 – I practice role-playing to better handle **objections** . . .1   2   3   4   5

23 – I daily practice my **closing** skills . . . . . . . . . . . . . . . .1   2   3   4   5

24 – I control my **temper** at all times . . . . . . . . . . . . . . . .1   2   3   4   5

## Section E – Personal Growth

25 – I am consistently receptive to **coaching** . . . . . . . . . . .1   2   3   4   5

26 – I invest in personal/**self-development** programs . . . . .1   2   3   4   5

27 – I'm able to receive **criticism** . . . . . . . . . . . . . . . . . . . .1   2   3   4   5

28 – I consider myself extremely **accountable.** . . . . . . . . . .1   2   3   4   5

29 – I consciously work on developing and acting on
     good working **habits** . . . . . . . . . . . . . . . . . . . . . . . . . .1   2   3   4   5

30 – I have a strong ability to **focus** on the task at hand . . .1   2   3   4   5

31 – When it comes to work chores and tasks, I am
     very **disciplined** . . . . . . . . . . . . . . . . . . . . . . . . . . . . .1   2   3   4   5

32 – I regularly **practice** scripts and dialogues . . . . . . . . . .1   2   3   4   5

33 – I refuse to **coast** through my job . . . . . . . . . . . . . . . . .1   2   3   4   5

34 – I am constantly pushing myself out of my
     current **comfort zone** . . . . . . . . . . . . . . . . . . . . . . . . .1   2   3   4   5

## Section F – Relationships

35 – As a rule of thumb, I do not believe in **trashing** others . .1  2  3  4  5

36 – I believe **gossip** tears people down . . . . . . . . . . . . . . .1  2  3  4  5

37 – I support this statement: "**Jealousy** gets me nowhere." . .1  2  3  4  5

38 – I **respect** my peers or bosses . . . . . . . . . . . . . . . . . . . . .1  2  3  4  5

39 – I support this statement: "**Greed** is never good." . . . . .1  2  3  4  5

40 – I am an **unselfish** person . . . . . . . . . . . . . . . . . . . . . . .1  2  3  4  5

41 – I've always been considered a strong **team** player . . . .1  2  3  4  5

42 – I don't believe in being **rude** to people . . . . . . . . . . . .1  2  3  4  5

43 – I believe that playing the **political** game
will never get you anywhere . . . . . . . . . . . . . . . . . . . . .1  2  3  4  5

44 – I'm able to keep my **ego** out of the big picture . . . . . .1  2  3  4  5

## Section G – Action Plans

45 – I'm very good at setting **priorities** . . . . . . . . . . . . . . . .1  2  3  4  5

46 – I'm known for my **organizational** skills . . . . . . . . . . .1  2  3  4  5

47 – I'm an excellent manager of my **time** . . . . . . . . . . . . .1  2  3  4  5

48 – I have consistent **energy** throughout the day . . . . . . .1  2  3  4  5

49 – My sales call **activity** is consistent and normally
on an upswing . . . . . . . . . . . . . . . . . . . . . . . . . . . . . . . .1  2  3  4  5

50 – I'm a strong **decision** maker and rarely regret
the decisions I've made . . . . . . . . . . . . . . . . . . . . . . . .1  2  3  4  5

51 – I like to **prospect** and do it very consistently . . . . . . .1  2  3  4  5

52 – I always **follow-up** on my commitments with my
clients and prospects . . . . . . . . . . . . . . . . . . . . . . . . . .1  2  3  4  5

## Section H – Staying on Course

53 – I'm quite capable of handling sudden **change** . . . . . .1  2  3  4  5

54 – I'm known for my **flexibility** . . . . . . . . . . . . . . . . .1  2  3  4  5

55 – I can control my **impulsive** desires . . . . . . . . . . . . .1  2  3  4  5

56 – I consistently avoid **procrastinating** . . . . . . . . . . . .1  2  3  4  5

57 – I do not allow **distractions** to get in the way of
my workday . . . . . . . . . . . . . . . . . . . . . . . . . .1  2  3  4  5

58 – People would never refer to me as
a **spendthrift** . . . . . . . . . . . . . . . . . . . . . . . . . .1  2  3  4  5

59 – I constantly work hard at building my
**resourcefulness** . . . . . . . . . . . . . . . . . . . . . . . . .1  2  3  4  5

60 – I take **pride** in my daily work and profession . . . . . . .1  2  3  4  5

61 – I've learned to handle **rejection** well . . . . . . . . . . . . .1  2  3  4  5

62 – I'm good at handling, saving and balancing my
**money** needs . . . . . . . . . . . . . . . . . . . . . . . . . .1  2  3  4  5

63 – I would consider myself **competitive** . . . . . . . . . . . . .1  2  3  4  5

64 – I am consistently **persistent** . . . . . . . . . . . . . . . . . .1  2  3  4  5

65 – My **perseverance** toward tasks is well-known
and recognized . . . . . . . . . . . . . . . . . . . . . . . . .1  2  3  4  5

66 – I'm always **hungry** for more! . . . . . . . . . . . . . . . . . .1  2  3  4  5

**Your call to action:**
1. Now it is time to add up your score.
2. Make a decision as to which chapters you will focus on for personal self-development.
3. See the next section – "My Sales Act."
4. Go to www.respectfactor.com and download your free copy of "My Sales Act."
5. Complete "My Sales Act" for each area of concern you have chosen for improved results.
6. Make a commitment to convert each area of concern to an advantage.

**Fully utilize *Jack, You're Fired!*; Your score will rise exponentially.**

# MY SALES ACT

## Focused Self Improvement Moves You Up the Ladder of Success

**SALES** = Sales Act Learning Experiences Success
**ACT** = Accountability Control Team

_____        _____
Sales Professional                      Date

_____        _____
Sales Coach                             Date

**Area of Concern** _____

_____

**My Action Plan** _____

_____

**Expected Result** _____

_____

**Assistance Needed** _____

_____

**Review Opportunity** (use reverse as needed)

| Date | Comments | Sales Professional | Sales Coach |
|------|----------|--------------------|-------------|
| ____ | _____ | _____ | _____ |
| ____ | _____ | _____ | _____ |
| ____ | _____ | _____ | _____ |
| ____ | _____ | _____ | _____ |

**P.S.** Celebrate when you have successfully converted your area of concern into an advantage.

© 2005 by Jack Perry